THE TROJAN HERITAGE

A PICTORIAL HISTORY OF USC FOOTBALL

O.J. Simpson rushes against Indiana on the way to a 14-3 win in the 1968 Rose Bowl and the national championship.

ARNOLD FRANKEL

USC adds three points in a 33-0 thrashing of old rival
Occidental in 1927. Note the cross-body blocking in the
center of the action.

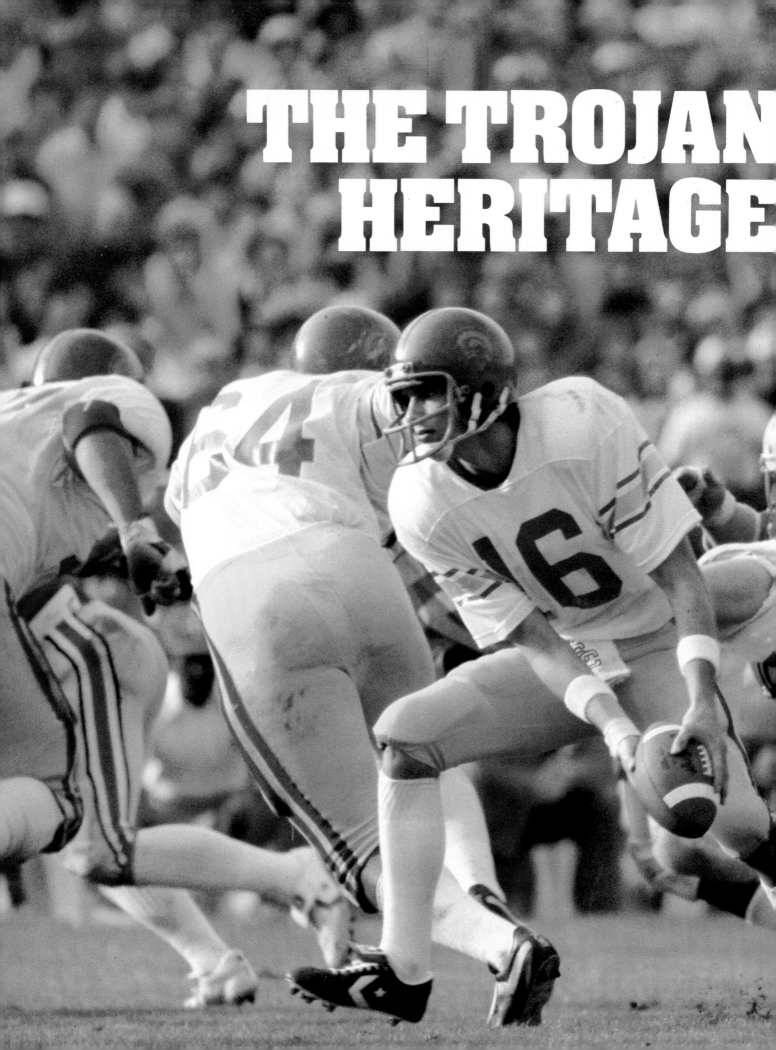

THE TROJAN HERITAGE

PICTORIAL HISTORY
OF USC FOOTBALL

BY MAL FLORENCE

JCP CORP. OF VIRGINIA

Quickness and sharp cutting were trademarks of Mike Garrett's running style as demonstrated in this 1963 action against Stanford.

PHOTO BY GARFIELD STUDIOS COURTESY OF USC SPORTS INFORMATION

Library of Congress Catalogue Number 80-84556
ISBN 0-938694-01-4

JCP Corp. of Virginia
214 40th Street
P.O. Box 814
Virginia Beach, Virginia 23451

CONTENTS

All-American guard Pat Howell escorts All-American tailback Charles White. A dozen times in the 1960s and 1970s, USC offensive linemen have been honored as All-Americans, which is one big reason USC has had so many All-American tailbacks.

ARNOLD FRANKEL

ROBERT PARKER

Looking as much like hand-to-hand combat as football, the Trojan and Irish lines go at each other in the 1976 version of college football's greatest series.

USC has had only one three-time All-American in its storied history. His name is Richard Wood, linebacker. The Trojans' record during his career (1972-74) — 31-3-2 and two national championships.

PROLOGUE

The stocky man with the trim build was counseling a USC tailback on the practice field. With gestures and in a quiet voice, he was telling the running back how to hit a certain hole, what the play meant and how best to utilize his ability.

But in a sense, by his presence, Mike Garrett was conveying to the Trojan tailback that they were both part of a proud tradition — a bond that has made football at the University of Southern California something special over the years.

Garrett, the model for the modern USC tailbacks and the school's first Heisman Trophy winner, was just visiting the campus. He had left USC 15 years before, but on his return this day, it was as if time stood still for a while.

Memories? Not necessarily.

"Nostalgia to me doesn't bring back experiences but just that good feeling," Garrett says. "When I think of USC, I get a warmth."

On any given day on the practice field or in the Coliseum locker room after a game, Mike Garrett, O.J. Simpson, or some other renowned player from another era will be there — sharing the exuberance of the moment and tacitly serving as a reminder of USC's athletic heritage.

The Trojan football tradition. It means many things:

• The teams. The Thundering Herd teams of the late 1920s and 1930s, the war babies of the mid 1940s, and the "I" formation-styled national champions of the 1960s and 1970s.

• The Rose Bowl, USC's second home.

• The tailback. The slot that has evolved into *the position* in college football. A glamour figure with names like Morley Drury, The Noblest Trojan of Them All in the late 1920s, and Russ Saunders, Gus Shaver, Orv Mohler, Cotton Warburton, Amby Schindler, Grenny Lansdell, Frank Gifford, Jon Arnett, Mike Garrett, O.J. Simpson, Anthony Davis, Ricky Bell and Charles White.

• The coaches who have made an indelible impression on the game. Gloomy Gus Henderson bringing national recognition to USC; Howard Jones earning national respect with his Rose Bowl-winning teams and national

champions; John McKay altering the concept of offensive football with his innovative "I" formation and John Robinson achieving that awesome balance of power running and productive passing, blended with stifling defense.

• The rivalries. The one with Notre Dame that began in 1926 and has grown into the most prestigious intersectional confrontation in the country. Then there's the one with UCLA, in which the outcome not only rewards the winner with bragging rights for the city, but also usually means a berth in the Rose Bowl.

• The games. The 16-14 victory over Notre Dame at South Bend in 1931 and the ensuing ticker tape parade in Los Angeles for the conquering heroes. The stunning 7-3 victory over Duke in the 1939 Rose Bowl. O.J. Simpson's climactic 64-yard touchdown run that beat UCLA, 21-20, in 1967 . . . and on and on.

• The Coliseum. USC's home since 1923. Here the latest Trojan horse, Traveler III, gallops around the track with rider Richard Saukko as the USC band stirs the crowd with its famous fight song, Fight On.

• And Heritage Hall, USC's athletic building where busts of famous coaches and Heisman Trophy winners are viewed daily by visitors.

All of this is USC football.

There's nothing like it.

Some things have changed — uniforms, playing surfaces, crowd sizes — others have remained the same — the Trojan tailback running behind power blocking — since USC began playing the game of football. This action is from USC's 1916 season-opening 14-0 win over the Sherman Indians.

Chapter One
IN A MUSTARD FIELD

In 1944 Harry C. Lillie, an attorney, visited Arnold Eddy, then the University of Southern California's manager of athletics, and supplied missing information on the school's first football team in 1888.

Existing records acknowledge that a team did exist eight years after the small Methodist school was founded in 1880, but there was no reference to any games that the team played.

Lillie revealed that the University of Southern California was undefeated in 1888 in a two-game schedule. How fitting this was for a school which, in the centennial year of its founding, has had almost unparalleled success in athletics — football, of course, and 63 NCAA championships, more by far than any other university in the country.

Lillie, a 125-pound end on the first ragtag USC team, told his story to Braven Dyer of the Los Angeles Times:

"The only available opposition was a club team which carried the name of Alliance. Our first game was Nov. 14, 1888, right at the university and we won by a score of 16-0.

"In those days a touchdown scored four points, with the play which now corresponds to the conversion after touchdown adding two more points. A field goal scored five points, while a safety scored two.

"The second game against Alliance was played more than two months later on Jan. 19, 1889, uptown on a vacant field bordered by Grand, Hope, Eighth and Ninth streets. The club team had improved considerably and we managed to score only a single touchdown to win, 4-0."

Frank Suffel and Henry H. Goddard were playing coaches for this first team which was literally put together by quarterback Arthur Carroll. He volunteered to make the pants for the team. Appropriately, Carroll later became a tailor in Riverside.

The growth of USC and its football program coincides with the growth of Los Angeles, which had been founded only 99 years before the cornerstone was laid at the university. The school was located, the Los Angeles Daily Herald noted, on "a vast stretch of unoccupied, uncultivated plain covered with a rank growth of mustard."

At the time, Los Angeles still retained some characteristics of its earlier pueblo days. "The old and new of Los Angeles were strangely blended," wrote Manuel P. Servin and Iris Higbie Wilson in their book, *Southern California and Its University*. "Thick walled adobes with large enclosed patios were still found in many parts of town to recall the early days, but brick, stone and frame houses were becoming the most popular.

". . . Beyond the business center there lingered a succession of orange groves and grape vineyards, walnut, almond and fruit orchards, and luxurious vegetable and flower gardens — a sight which caused enthusiastic visitors to liken Los Angeles to a veritable 'Garden of Paradise'."

It was in this setting that USC had its humble beginnings as a university. There was no way to envision that the football team that beat the Alliance Athletic Club would be the precursor of Howard Jones' famed Thundering Herd teams, John McKay's sophisticated "I"-formation-styled national champions and, now, John Robinson's successful teams.

American football at the turn of the century was a combination of rugby, soccer and pure mayhem. The rules provided for a playing field of 110 yards in length, exclusive of the end zones, and games were played in 45-minute halves with a 10-minute intermission.

Intentional tackling below the waist, a fundamental and coached procedure now, was judged a foul then, just like unnecessary roughness.

USC fielded another team in 1889 (without a coach) and encountered its first collegiate opponent, St. Vincent's, now known as Loyola-Marymount. The Methodists or Wesleyans (the name Trojans would come later) thrashed St. Vincent's, 40-0, and then beat a Pasadena club team which featured the dreaded Flying Wedge, 26-0.

So far, so good. A pair of two-game seasons and USC was undefeated, untied and unscored upon.

Then, because of student apathy and some

financial problems, USC didn't have a team in 1890.

A pattern developed in which USC, still coachless, would play a one- to four-game schedule — without much success — until 1897 when Lewis Freeman became the school's first non-playing coach. Not only did he outfit the team in sharp, new uniforms — turtle-necked shirts with "USC" inscribed on the front, knee-length pants and ankle-high shoes — he produced a winning team with a then-representative schedule.

USC, under Freeman, won five of its six games, losing only to the San Diego YMCA, 18-0. Freeman then moved on, but the Methodists continued their winning ways, recording a 5-1-1 record in 1898 — losing to and being tied by Los Angeles High School.

Losing to a prep school wasn't too embarrassing then; L.A. High was beating major universities, including California, a recognized power to the north.

It was during the late 1890s and the early 1900s that USC developed a rivalry with neighboring Occidental and Pomona, the early stand-ins for Notre Dame, California and Stanford.

Paul Lowry, a former Los Angeles Times sports editor, recalled with amusement a 1904 game between Occidental and USC in a story he wrote years later for the Pigskin Review, USC's football magazine:

"USC won, 36-4, but you'll smile when I tell you the boys played only 25 minutes. The officials were members of the rival schools and, when they got through debating about the rules, there was little time to play and the game was called because of darkness."

The year 1904 also marked the arrival of Harvey Holmes, the first salaried USC coach. He stayed four years, compiled a record of 19 wins, five losses and three ties and expanded USC's schedule to 10 games in 1905, including a first meeting with Stanford. USC lost that game, 16-0, as one of the West Coast's most prestigious rivalries began. The teams wouldn't meet again in football until 1918.

Major college teams do not schedule too many "breathers" today because of financial considerations. But USC wasn't thinking of the gate when it padded its 6-3-1 record in 1905 with victories over the likes of the National Guard, Whittier Reform and the Alumni.

At the same time that Holmes was

establishing USC as a formidable football team in the southern part of the state, California and Stanford were abandoning the game in favor of rugby. Educators at some universities said that football was too brutal a game and even the White House looked with disfavor on the sport. President Theodore Roosevelt, angered by a photograph of a battered player, said, in effect, that unless unnecessarily rough play was eliminated, the game would have to be abolished.

USC continued to play football in 1908 under coach Bill Traeger. In 1909 and 1910 the team was under a coach who was to become famous in another sport.

Dean Bartlett Cromwell was called the "Maker of Champions" during his 40 years at USC — track and field champions, that is.

A legendary figure in track and field, Cromwell's teams won 12 NCAA titles including nine in a row from 1935 through 1943.

His track teams also won eight Pacific Coast Conference championships and a few IC4A titles. He produced at least one Olympic champion in each of the Games from 1912 through 1948.

Cromwell was a master psychologist and, with his ever-present bow tie neatly in place, he had a standard greeting for all of his athletes, whether outstanding or mediocre: "Hi Champ. How are you doing? I know you can win."

Some say he was a con artist, but no matter. Seldom has any track coach been as successful as "The Dean" and, when he retired in 1948, he became the U.S. Olympic track and field coach.

As a football coach, Cromwell had only modest success with 3-1-2 and 7-0-1 records in 1909 and 1910 and later a three-year record of 11-7-3 when he served as USC's football coach from 1916 through 1918.

Between Cromwell's first and second terms as football coach (along with a two-year tenure by Ralph Glaze, 1914-15), USC decided to move up in class athletically.

Rugby, as played by California and Stanford, was USC's game in 1911 and a school spokesman said, "We are looking for a foothold on an athletic ladder that would carry us, we hoped, to a level of competition to the proportion of our ambitious, restless, growing young institution."

The results were disastrous, according to

Dean Cromwell, shown here in his playing days at Occidental, was the first coach to bring real stability to the USC football program. He coached the team for five years (1909-1910, 1916-1918), his term being interrupted by the school's flirtation with rugby and two years by Ralph Glaze. The football post was just a way-station, however, on his way to an unparalleled career as USC track coach.

USC powers for the goal in a 31-6 win over Arizona to open the 1917 season. The helmets of the day look like little more than caps with ear muffs.

Servin and Wilson in their book, *Southern California and Its University*. USC was badly outclassed for three years (1911-13) by more experienced rugby teams. It suffered financial reverses as well.

But all was not lost in this departure from American football. The Methodist school that was founded in a mustard field got a nickname that would identify it and its students and alumni glamorously for years to come.

Nicknames were popular in the early 1900s, but the school didn't care much to be called Methodists or Wesleyans. So Owen R. Bird, a sportswriter for the Los Angeles Times, came up with a nickname that was to endure.

Bird's article of Feb. 24, 1912, read: "The Oxy Tiger will be seen in action . . . in the clash with Dean Cromwell's U.S.C. Trojans on the Bovard cinder trail. Speculation is running rife as to the outcome of the meet at both colleges."

It was Bird's belief that "owing to the terrific

The 1915 backfield featured (l-r) Frank Malette, Leonard Livernash and Gerald Craig. Malette was considered the best back USC had produced in his time, while Livernash captained the 1915 squad.

handicaps under which the athletes, coaches and managers of the university were laboring and against the overwhelming odds of larger and better equipped rivals, the name 'Trojan' suitably fitted the players."

It obviously did.

When USC began playing football again in 1914, it also resumed its relationship with Occidental and Pomona. But the Trojans wanted to be known beyond the limited confines of Bovard Field (named after USC president George F. Bovard), so they began to schedule "big-time" opponents such as St. Mary's, Oregon and California which had resumed football in 1915.

USC split with California in 1915, winning, 28-10, and losing 23-21. Another traditional series was inaugurated.

World War I put a damper on USC's athletic ambitions and the school played a restricted schedule from 1917 through 1919. Harold Galloway, acting captain of the 1918 team, noted the unusual circumstances of the season when he wrote in the El Rodeo, the school's yearbook:

". . . The government was in control of the athletic program and the primary object of the government in establishing the S.A.T.C. was to train men in the fundamentals of military tactics and life . . . the men were also compelled to keep up with their studies in order to pass their examinations prior to being sent to an O.T.C. Hence, a very limited time was allowed for practice.

"Then we had this season friend influenza and influenza right through the football team. It was impossible to keep the team intact . . . the men were looking forward to the day when Uncle Sam would call them to colors. They were far more interested in toting the gun against the Hun than making flying tackles and snagging forward passes."

USC had some outstanding football players during its formative years, athletes such as Elwin Caley (whose 107-yard punt return in 1902 on a 110-yard field still stands as a school record), Hal Paulin, Arthur Hill, Roy Allan, Court Decius, Fred Kelly, Fred Teschke, Rabbit Malette, Tank Campbell, Turk Hunter, Dan McMillan and Herb Jones.

But the Trojans wouldn't become nationally recognized in football to some extent until the 1920s. USC had a bright future, even though its first big-time coach would become renowned for his pessimism.

The Trojans work on their kicking game prior to their 1916 game against Utah.

USC's single wing starts left in this action against Pomona in 1916. The small shoulder pads and oversized ball show football's close kinship to rugby at the time.

Elmer C. "Gloomy Gus" Henderson coached the Trojans to a 45-7 record during his six-year tenure (1919-1924) at USC — a winning percentage second only to that recently attained by John Robinson.

Chapter Two
"GLOOMY" ONLY IN NAME

Until John Robinson moved into the No. 1 position in 1979 with a career record of 42-6-1 (.867), Elmer C. (Gloomy Gus) Henderson had the best winning percentage, 45-7 (.865), of any coach in USC's history.

Better than the legendary Howard Jones. Better than John McKay, who won four national championships.

More importantly than his percentage, Henderson, in his five seasons at the school (1919-1924), achieved a semblance of national recognition for USC and established the format for successful teams of the future.

It was under Henderson that USC recorded some historic firsts:

• Appearing in the Rose Bowl in 1923 and beating Penn State, 14-3.

• Winning 10 games in a season twice, along with an undefeated season in 1920 (with a schedule that would be soft by modern standards, but considerably better than back-to-back meetings with the Alliance AC).

And it was under Henderson that USC moved out of Bovard Field, where a turnaway crowd would be 10,000, to play in the vast Memorial Coliseum, where crowds of 70,000 would become routine for Trojan games.

Henderson was the first USC coach to recruit aggressively and he persuaded talented Southern California athletes to stay home and attend USC rather than to pursue their education at California or Stanford.

He also was an on-the-field innovator. His spread formations were copied by coaches and some elements of his offense are used today by college teams and the NFL.

Ironically, Henderson was fired and paid off at the end of the 1924 season.

Some say that he was released because he couldn't beat California's Wonder Teams during his tenure, although he never lost to Stanford.

Others say that California and Stanford officials pressured USC to drop Henderson because of his recruiting policies. Cal even

Old rival Occidental was having a tough time keeping up with USC by 1921 when USC prevailed, 42-0. Notice the noseguard on the player at the far left.

broke off relations with USC for one year.

For whatever reason, Henderson occupies an enigmatic place in USC's football history.

He came to USC from Broadway High School in Seattle, where his teams had a four-year record of 24-2-1 and outscored their opponents, 586 to 84.

He brought some of the talented members from the high school team with him, including Leo Calland, an outstanding lineman for USC from 1920 through 1922.

"Gloomy Gus" was a well-known cartoon character of the era and Henderson was saddled with that nickname by Los Angeles Times sports writer, Paul Lowry, because of the way he poor-mouthed the Trojans' prospects before a game.

Henderson, before a 1919 game with favored Pomona, told Lowry that USC's line was so full of holes that it would make a Swiss cheese blush, that his center was not the center of the line but merely the center of gloom and sorrow, and that his backs couldn't find a hole in the line if it was as large as Los Angeles' Second Street tunnel.

When USC went on to upset Pomona, 6-0, then beat Stanford, 13-0, and tax strong California before losing, 14-13, sportswriters became understandably leery of Henderson's dire pronouncements. In truth, Henderson, a graduate of Oberlin College in Ohio, was a congenial person and an engaging storyteller.

It has been reported that Henderson had only 26 players at his first practice in 1919. That year USC's enrollment was less than 4,000 compared to 14,000 at California.

Nevertheless, USC had a 4-1 record in 1919, went undefeated in 1920 (without playing Cal) and was 10-1 in 1921 and again in 1922, two seasons in which the Trojans outscored their opposition, 598 to 83.

The Navy helped enhance USC's record in those two years as the Trojans swamped the USS Arizona, USS New York, Sub Base and USS Mississippi (the games counted) by scores of 62-0, 35-0, 34-0 and 20-0.

USC had a 6-2 record in 1923 which included the first football game ever to be played in the Coliseum — a 23-7 win over Pomona on October 6 — and a later Coliseum game, a 13-7

USC opened the 1923 season playing in front of a few fans and the old physical education building. By season's end they had played in front of more than 250,000 people in their new home at the L.A. Coliseum. This 18-7 win over Cal Tech was the last game played at Bovard Field.

loss to Cal, that attracted 72,000 fans and dramatically sent a signal to Easterners that football on the West Coast had *really* caught on.

Henderson had a 9-2 record in his last season at USC in 1924, a year that featured intersectional games with Syracuse and Missouri, both of which the Trojans won.

The same 1924 season, the Trojans learned at Berkeley that California and Stanford didn't want to have anything more to do with the upstart Methodist school in Los Angeles. USC had been admitted into the Pacific Coast Conference in 1922, but California and Stanford in particular didn't approve of Henderson's recruiting methods or of USC's academic or eligibility standards.

Just before the USC-Cal game at Berkeley in 1924, the president of the California Associated Students informed the USC student body president by a hand-delivered letter that California and Stanford were severing athletic relations with USC at the end of the football season.

Gwynn Wilson, USC's graduate manager at

USC's explosive offense demoralizes Arizona as the Trojans waltz to a 69-6 victory in 1923.

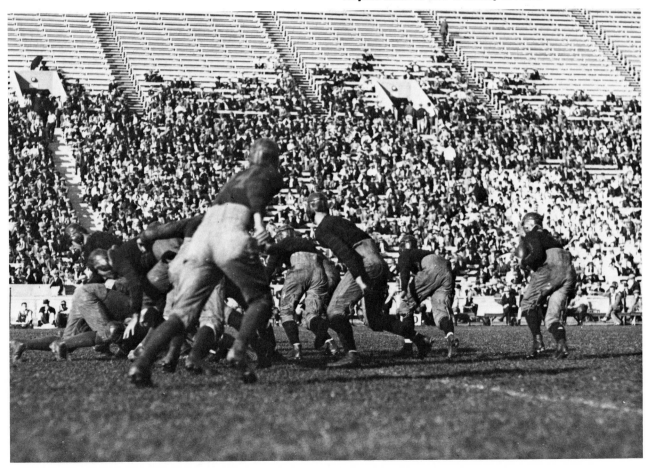

the time (a position similar to today's athletic director), recalls the incident vividly:

"I was called into an office at Berkeley just before the game and told by the Cal graduate manager and his assistant that California and Stanford were going to break with us after the game," Wilson said. "They said, 'We like you, Gwynn, but not your university.' I immediately told Harold Stonier (USC vice president) about it and we had to decide whether we were even going to play the game against Cal."

USC decided to play and was further humiliated by losing to Cal, 7-0, for the fourth straight year.

"However, we cancelled the Stanford game that was scheduled the very next week and played St. Mary's instead," Wilson said. "If they (Stanford) didn't want to play us, we didn't want to play them."

Wilson surmises that California and Stanford's action came about because the northern schools believed that USC was getting too strong too fast in football.

As for USC's reported illegal recruiting tactics, Wilson said, "There were no rules in those days. It was an open season (recruiting)

situation. We weren't any worse or any better in that regard than anyone else."

California wasn't on USC's schedule in 1925, but, curiously, Stanford was back on it.

Wilson explained: "A lot of Stanford people didn't like the idea of breaking with USC. They felt that Cal took the lead and pushed them into it. Stanford alums got up in arms and put things back together."

But things couldn't be put back together for "Gloomy Gus" Henderson, who was on his way out. Wilson recalled that Henderson was being paid $10,000 annually and he was given a check for $20,000 at the end of the season to terminate his six-year coaching career at USC.

Wilson said that dissatisfaction with Henderson began after previously unbeaten USC lost to California at Berkeley in 1921. Andy Smith's Wonder Team, led by the famous Brick Muller, surprised the Trojans with a passing attack and won easily, 38-7.

"It was like the screen passes we have today," Wilson said. "And Henderson never adjusted. When we got back on 'the Yale' for the 18-hour boat trip back to Los Angeles, a lot of alums were already grumbling about Henderson."

The 1923 edition of the Trojans holds Nevada scoreless en route to a 33-0 victory and a 6-2 season.

Ed Green held the USC kickoff return record — 98 yards against Cal Tech in 1924 — for fifty years until it was finally broken by Anthony Davis.

Regarded by some as Henderson's best team, the 1924 Trojans gained national recognition following their 16-0 triumph over formidable Syracuse.

('The Yale' and 'the Harvard' serviced Los Angeles and the Bay area in those days and alums chartered the boats for the football trips.)

Los Angeles sportswriters, such as Braven Dyer, Sid Ziff, Paul Zimmerman and Maxwell Stiles, would write in later years that Henderson lost his job because of politics. They all agreed that the innovative coach with the pessimistic nickname put USC on the nation's football map, to use the cliche of the time.

Henderson went on to become a successful coach at Tulsa, the Los Angeles Bulldogs (which was an exciting, independent professional team with a diversified, spread formation offense), the Detroit Lions and Occidental. He died in Palm Springs in 1965 at the age of 76.

During his tenure at USC, Henderson recruited and developed such outstanding players as Chet Dolley, Harold Galloway, Johnny Leadingham, Charley Dean, Roy (Bullet) Baker, Gordon Campbell, Andy Toolen, Lowell Lindley, Hobo Kincaid, Indian Newman, Hobbs Adams, Hayden Phythian, Holley Adams, Norman Anderson, Otto Anderson, Johnny Hawkins, Hank Lefebvre, Eddie Leahy, Manuel Laraneta, Butter Gorrell, Jeff Cravath and Calland.

Two of Henderson's sophomores on the 1924 squad, guard Brice Taylor and quarterback Mort Kaer, would later become USC's first All-Americans. Henderson is credited with recruiting Morley Drury, who would become known as the "Noblest Trojan of them All."

The "Gloomy Gus" nickname aside, Henderson was an outgoing person who had a rapport with his players. His successor, Howard Jones, was more introverted and aloof than Henderson. But during Jones' 16 years as USC's coach, the Trojans would attain a level of excellence matched by very few schools in the country.

As famous as Jones became, a more famous coach almost succeeded Henderson in 1925.

The highlight of the Henderson era was probably the 14-3 win over Penn State in the 1923 Rose Bowl. Not only was it USC's first appearance in the "granddaddy of the bowl games," it was also the first time the classic was played at its present location.

The 1924 team gathers for a group shot before the season finale against Missouri. Little did they realize this would be Coach Henderson's (far left) last game as he was dismissed following this season.

Chapter Three
"HEADMAN"

The course of college football history might have been changed radically if Notre Dame's Knute Rockne had become USC's coach following Henderson's release before the 1925 season.

Such an idea was neither improbable nor fanciful. It came close to becoming a reality. Gwynn Wilson, the USC graduate manager in the 1920s, remembers:

"Rockne came to USC for a football seminar and we saw a lot of him. We didn't have a coach and we talked to Rock about the job. He agreed to come, subject to getting a release from Notre Dame. Mrs. Rockne had fallen in love with Southern California. We had hopes but they (Notre Dame) talked him into staying. Maybe it was better that Rock stayed there and we got Jones."

Howard Harding Jones. Known as the Headman. Responsible for bringing national recognition to USC at a time when the East and Midwest were considered the twin citadels of college football.

A quiet and almost austere man who probably would have become more renowned had he been as flamboyant as Rockne, Jones subscribed to — and upheld — the old-fashioned virtues. He didn't drink. "Gad darn it" was his strongest profanity.

His approach to the game was straight-forward yet intricate — power football, the single wing. Opponents often said they knew where the Trojans, under Jones, were coming, but still couldn't stop them. Jones' teams became known as the Thundering Herd, running (seldom passing) roughshod over some of the nation's best teams.

Before Jones came to USC, the school had not produced an All-American or won a national championship. During his 16 years as USC's coach, Jones developed 19 All-Americans, won national championships in 1928, 1931 and 1932, had undefeated seasons in 1928, 1932 and 1939, won eight Pacific Coast Conference titles and was undefeated in five appearances in the Rose Bowl.

His overall record was 121-36-13 (.750) and his teams had seven seasons in which they won nine or more games.

It was during Jones' regime, in 1926, that the USC-Notre Dame rivalry began, a rivalry now esteemed as the most prestigious intersectional series in the country.

The Trojan tailback is almost a cult figure today. USC football is irrevocably identified

BRICE UNION TAYLOR

1902 – 1974

FIRST USC ALL-AMERICAN FOOTBALL PLAYER

UNIVERSITY OF SOUTHERN CALIFORNIA FROM 1923 TO 1926

"AIM HIGH, BELIEVE YOURSELF CAPABLE OF GREAT THINGS -- YOU WILL SUCCEED"

This plaque honoring Brice Taylor holds a place of honor in Heritage Hall on the USC campus. Taylor was the first of more than 70 All-Americans to star for the Trojans.

Howard Jones was one of the all-time coaching giants, compiling a 121-36-13 record from 1925-1940 at USC. He built the Trojans into one of the game's dominant teams, winning three national championships and five Rose Bowls. Jones believed in fundamental, power football and his "Thundering Herd" established the tradition of great running backs that is still a trademark of USC football. Although not as well known as his more flamboyant colleague, Knute Rockne, he was indisputably the "Headman."

Mort Kaer holds the distinction of being USC's first All-American tailback, winning the accolade in 1926. More than a dozen Trojan tailbacks have been so honored.

The "Herd" thunders on a power sweep off right tackle, Howard Jones' favorite play, in a big 1925 win over Montana. The win was one of 11 in Jones' first year. All-American Brice Taylor leads the blocking in the center of the line.

with Frank Gifford, Jon Arnett, Mike Garrett, O.J. Simpson, Anthony Davis, Ricky Bell and Charles White. Jones developed the prototype of the modern tailback. His tailback, called the quarterback in the Jones' system, not only carried the ball 80 or 90 percent of the time, but also passed, punted and played safety on defense.

These running backs weren't Toms, Dicks or Harrys — they had a certain regal quality to their names: Morton Kaer, Morley Drury, Russ Saunders, Marshall Duffield, Gaius (Gus) Shaver, Orville Mohler, Homer Griffith, Irvine (Cotton) Warburton, Ambrose Schindler and Grenville Lansdell.

There was the great blocking back, Erny Pinckert, and later Bob Hoffman. The linemen of the 20s and 30s were the best of their day — Brice Taylor, Jesse Hibbs, Nate Barragar, Francis Tappaan, Garrett Arbelbide, Johnny Baker, Stan Williamson, Tay Brown, Ernie Smith, Aaron Rosenberg and Harry Smith.

Jones made an immediate impact at USC. His first team in 1925 had an 11-2 record, losing just to Stanford and Washington State. The Trojans were 8-2 in 1926, 8-1-1 in 1927, 9-0-1 in 1928, 10-2 in 1929 and 8-2 in 1930. After a season-opening loss to St. Mary's in 1931, the Trojans didn't lose another game until Stanford beat them, 13-7, in 1933 — a 27-game unbeaten streak.

Trojan old timers still argue about which team was Jones' best. Some say it was the 1929 team that destroyed Pittsburgh in the Rose Bowl, 47-14, even though USC lost two regular season games. Others contend it was the 1931 club that rebounded from the loss to St. Mary's to go undefeated the rest of the season, including the historic 16-14 upset of Notre Dame at South Bend.

For the purists who say that the record is the only way to measure the worth of a team, it's difficult to dispute the credentials of the 1932 team, which went 10-0 and allowed its opponents to score only 13 points.

As usually happens to any coach who has a long association with a single school, Jones had some down years, from 1934 through 1937. Disgruntled alumni began to say that the Headman couldn't keep up with the modern concepts of the game.

USC rebounded with a 9-2 record in 1938, including a 7-3 Rose Bowl victory over Duke in which fourth-string quarterback Doyle Nave came off the bench in the final minutes to throw four consecutive passes to end "Antelope" Al Krueger, the last for the touchdown. The Blue Devils went into the Rose Bowl undefeated, untied and unscored upon.

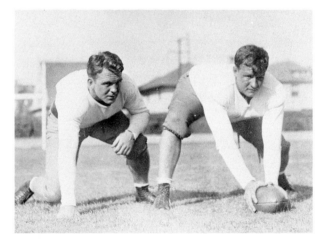

Nate Barragar (left) and George Dye were two of the standouts in the Trojans' 1929 line. Barragar was team captain, and his jarring style earned All-America notices.

Legendary Stanford Coach "Pop" Warner (left) and Christy Walsh (right) congratulate Erny Pinckert on his All-American selection in 1930. The colorful, rugged Pinckert was one of the few backs ever selected as an All-American on his blocking ability alone.

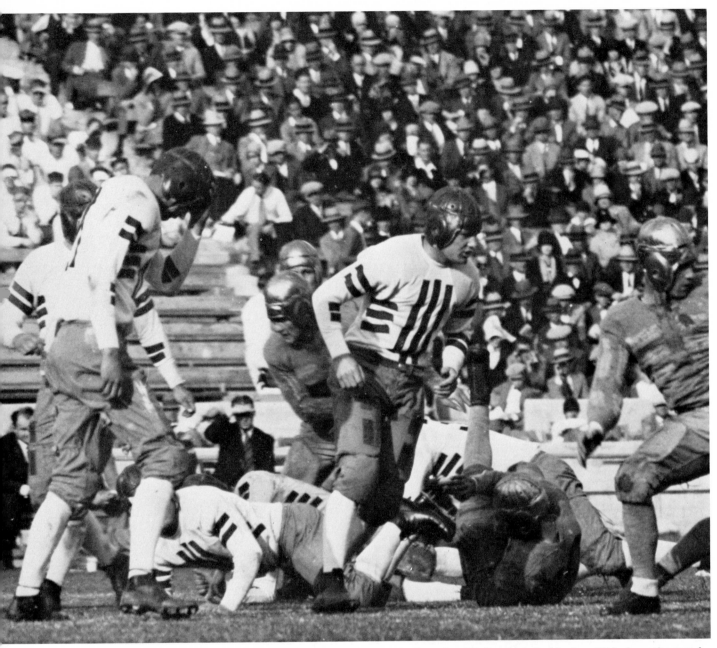

Two-time All-American tackle Jess Hibbs is on the prowl against Colorado in 1927.

Some insist that Jones' last great team in 1939 was his best. USC was unbeaten, but tied by Oregon and UCLA, in 10 games. The Trojans climaxed the season with Jones' final Rose Bowl victory, 14-0, over Tennessee. Tennessee, like Duke, went into the Rose Bowl unscored upon in 1939. This game featured four All-Americans.

This was a USC team made up of Lansdell, Schindler, Nave, Bob Peoples, Jack Banta, Hoffman, Joe Shell, Harry Smith, Ray George, Bob Winslow, Howard Stoecker, Ed Dempsey and Ben Sohn — all accomplished athletes.

Jones died of a heart attack July 27, 1941, at the age of 55. The Trojans would have some strong teams in the next 20 years under four coaches, but they wouldn't win another national championship until the John McKay era.

A Yale man and a former All-American at that school along with his famous brother Tad, Jones was already a competent coach when he came to USC in 1925.

He had an auspicious coaching debut at the age of 23, leading Syracuse to a 6-3-1 record in 1908. He returned to Yale in 1909 and had an undefeated season and produced six All-Americans.

Then Jones was at Ohio State, back to Yale again, and then settling at Iowa from 1916 through 1923. His Iowa teams had a 42-17 record and undefeated seasons in 1921 and 1922. His rivalry with Rockne actually began at Iowa and he had the satisfaction of defeating Notre Dame, 10-7, in 1921 — ending a 21-game unbeaten string for Rockne's Fighting Irish.

After a season at Duke in which he had a 4-5 record with a weak team, Jones became USC's coach. Some say he got the job on the recommendation of Rockne.

Henderson had been reportedly fired, among other reasons, for not being able to defeat California. Jones took care of this detail. USC beat Cal, 27-0, in 1926 and lost to the Golden Bears only once in the next seven years. During this domination, the Trojans beat Cal, 74-0, in 1930, precipitating charges from the north of "professionalism" in USC athletics because the school reportedly paid its players. Nothing came of this verbal dispute.

Jones took a while, however, to get a bead on Stanford. Glenn (Pop) Warner, an old coaching adversary of Jones, was the Stanford coach and he beat USC 13-9 in 1925 and 13-12 in 1926 and was tied 13-13 in 1927 before Jones finally prevailed in his national championship season of 1928.

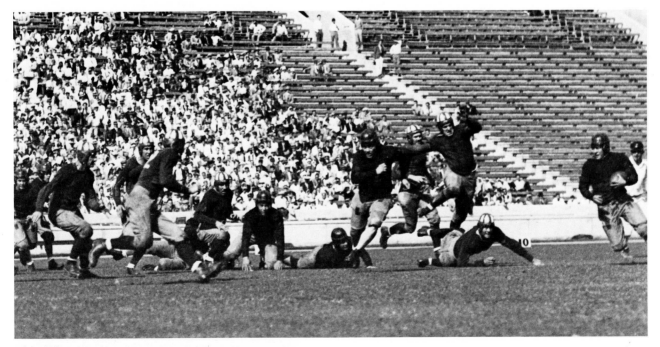

Don Williams heads upfield in the 1928 season-opening 40-12 win over Utah State, launching USC's drive to its first national championship. Williams led the Thundering Herd in rushing for the season.

Fran Tappaan makes a leaping catch and goes for the only touchdown in a 7-0 win over big rival Stanford in 1929. Tappaan earned All-American honors for his great play on what some considered Jones' best team.

USC's strong running game in 1928 was matched by a swarming defense, shown here surrounding a hapless Oregon State runner.

Braven Dyer wrote in his book, *Ten Top Trojan Thrillers,* that Warner was convinced he had one of his greatest teams at Stanford. Stanford had two big backs, Herb Fleishacker at 220 pounds and Biff Hoffman at 195 pounds, operating behind a huge line for that era.

Jones had ordered one of his assistants, Cliff Herd, to follow the Indians all year and from Herd's reports, Dyer wrote, the Headman formulated a plan to offset Stanford's 10-pound-per-man weight advantage.

"Once Pop's plays got rolling, the idea was to get in there immediately and start belting somebody," Dyer wrote. "They (USC) called it the 'quick mix' in those days. Perhaps it isn't very revolutionary as we look back, but for the most part, opposing teams up until the Jones plan had been content to sit back and wait for Pop's reverses to come to them. This, of course, was more or less fatal . . .

"Howard sent his ends and tackles crashing in immediately to batter down the interference. When the ballcarrier poked his head beyond the line of scrimmage he had been stripped clean, or nearly so, and hard-hitting secondary tacklers thus got a clear shot."

Jones' "quick mix" enabled USC to win, 10-0, with the crashing style of his defense forcing five Stanford fumbles, three of which were recovered by USC. Tackle Bob Hall and end Garrett Arbelbide were the defensive stars for USC and Harry Edelson, Russ Saunders and Lloyd Thomas were 60-minute men, not unusual in those days, in the backfield.

It was a landmark game for USC and Jones. Not only did the Trojans go on to an unbeaten season, but Warner never beat Jones again. The famous coach left Stanford at the end of the 1932 season.

The 1928 season also marked USC's first victory (27-14) over Notre Dame, after Rockne had tagged Jones with one-point defeats in 1926 and 1927.

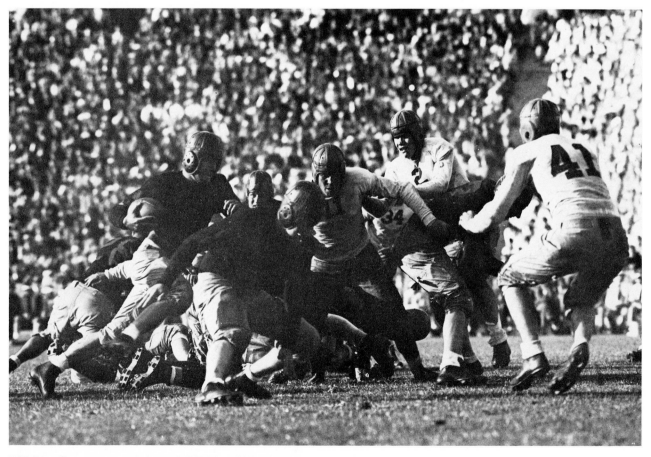

USC literally ran over and through UCLA in 1929, winning the first game in that storied series, 76-0. Small wonder this team was actually the first to be given the sobriquet "Thundering Herd."

Rockne would beat Jones two more times — 13-12 in 1929 and 27-0 in 1930 — when Bucky O'Connor, a substitute halfback playing fullback, ripped apart one of the Headman's best teams.

Rockne died in a plane crash March 31, 1931, leaving, among other memorable accomplishments, the foundation of the stirring Trojan-Irish series.

Jones had a remarkably consistent record from 1925 through 1933, never losing more than two games in a season and establishing USC's winning tradition in the Rose Bowl.

After being upset by St. Mary's, 13-7, in the 1931 opener, USC didn't lose another game (the 27-game unbeaten streak) until Stanford's Vow Boys beat the Trojans, 13-7, at the Coliseum. They were called Vow Boys because, as sophomores, they vowed that they would never lose to USC during their collegiate careers — and they didn't.

Although USC went on to finish the 1933 season with a 10-1-1 record, including a third straight victory over Notre Dame, it would be Jones' last strong team until the late 30s.

Jones, who previously never had a losing

This unusual 1929 publicicity photo features (l-r) "Racehorse" Russ Saunders, Rockwell Kemp, Erny Pinckert and their wives. Pinckert was a two-time All-American blocking back in 1930 and 1931. Saunders surprised Pitt with three TD passes in the 1930 Rose Bowl, after scoring 14 TDs himself during the season.

record at USC, fielded teams that went 4-6-1 in 1934, 5-7 in 1935, 4-2-3 in 1936 and 4-4-2 in 1937. No All-Americans. No Rose Bowl. The Thundering Herd, a nickname credited to sportswriter Maxwell Stiles, was idly grazing on the Coliseum grass.

Paul Zimmerman, a former sports editor of the Los Angeles Times, analyzed USC's decline:

"Howard had a lot of fine stars who spent three years on the bench when they could have played at some of the other schools. The high school players figured that out for themselves and many decided to go elsewhere. Of course, alumni and coaches at other schools were stepping up their recruiting. By the same token the Jones staff and the alumni naturally got to riding on their oars, assuming every great prep star would want to be a part of the 'Thundering Herd.'"

Jones stoically — and typically — endured sniping from the press and alumni during this down period, including an article by Charles Paddock, the former world's fastest human from USC, that said that Jones' system was obselete and he was nothing more than a character-builder.

But the Headman answered his critics by producing strong teams in 1938 and 1939. However, the Trojans slipped back into a 3-4-2 rut in 1940, the season before Jones died.

Al Wesson, the sports publicist at USC from 1928 through 1942, probably knew Jones as well as anyone could.

"It is probably trite to say it now," Wesson said, "but Jones was really a character-builder. He did what he thought was right, but he didn't preach to anyone. The players respected him, but he had very little contact with them except on the field."

Nick Pappas, who played quarterback for Jones in the mid-30s and is a USC associate athletic director in charge of athlete-support groups (namely, the influential Trojan Club), said that Jones didn't even have an office at the school.

"We saw him the first day of fall practice and, when the season ended, we didn't see him again until the following season," Pappas said.

Jones was so absorbed with football that he would get lost while driving to his home in North Hollywood. He was always thinking

Prof. Frank G. Dickinson (left) presents the Knute Rockne award to USC for winning its second national title in 1931. From left to right are Dickinson: Dr. Rufus B. VonKleinSmid. president of the university: Stanley Williamson. team captain: and coach Howard Jones.

about the game and Zimmerman once wrote:

"He was so wrapped up in the game that he always came back from trout fishing trips with his pockets crammed with grid notes. Those trips were easy on the fish but hard on the opponents next fall.

"He liked to play bridge but broke up many a foursome by drawing diagrams on the score pad or turning the session into a grid-iron clinic. He forgot luncheon dates, appointments and family commitments. But he never forgot anything when planning a defense against an opponent."

Howard Jones was called the "Headman" because when he took charge of practice sessions, that is exactly what he was. One of the players taking in Jones' instructions is a young John Wayne (standing, center).

Wesson is responsible for Jones' other name, the Headman.

"He didn't rely much on his assistants," Wesson said, "and when he wanted something done, he just took over. People would ask me what was going on and I'd say, 'See Howard, he's the headman.' Then everybody started calling him the Headman. He really was. It was a one-man show."

Wesson recalled an incident to make his point.

"As I said, he didn't listen much to his assistant coaches, except to Bill Hunter (who was also USC's athletic director from 1925 through 1957). In those days we didn't have assistant coaches sitting in the press box pouring information to the head coach on the sidelines.

" But one day he asked Sam Barry (USC's basketball coach who would become football coach for the 1941 season) to sit high in the end zone and see how the holes were opening up. I sat with Sam and he made a good chart of where we could go and who wasn't doing his job.

"Sam tried to impart this information to Howard at halftime. But Jones was busy talking to his quarterbacks and said, 'Never mind, Sam, tell me later.' At the start of the third quarter, Sam tried to get Howard's attention again to tell him of his scouting report. 'Just give me a minute,' Sam said. Howard replied: 'Is it really important? Tell me about it Monday.' "

Pappas said that Jones was a football genius who had total recall of every play of every game — even if he couldn't find his way home.

"He could stand on the sideline and he knew what everybody did — or should have done — on every play," Pappas said. "And, when he walked onto the practice field, the atmosphere changed immediately. You might be horsing around but, when he arrived, everybody went right to work without a word being said."

Jones believed in and coached power football. Although his Thundering Herd teams rolled up yardage and scored as many as 492 points as early as 1929, some critics incessantly carped that USC's offense was unimaginative.

Jones added wrinkles to his offense, to be sure. He made good use of a wingback reverse and a surprise passing attack, demonstrated to near-perfection in the 1930 Rose Bowl game when Russ Saunders threw three touchdown passes to beat Pittsburgh.

Two-time All-American Aaron Rosenberg helped anchor the 1932 defense that allowed just 13 points and no touchdowns by rushing on the way to a second successive national championship. He was equally adept at opening holes for Trojan running backs.

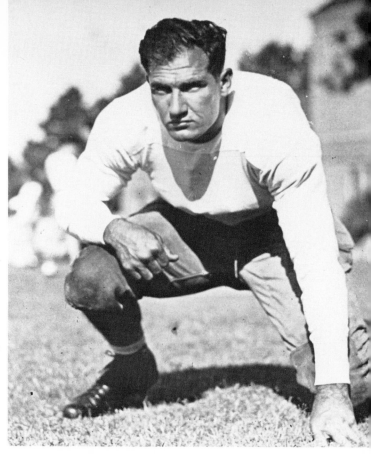

Ernie Smith was a devastating two-way tackle on the back-to-back national champs of 1931-32. He opened holes for All-American backs Orv Mohler, Erny Pinckert, Gus Shaver and "Cotton" Warburton, while his defensive play helped the Trojans earn the nickname, the "Whispering Herd," in 1932.

Still, it was the running game with flawless execution that was the trademark of Jones' best teams. Another coach in another era, the late Vince Lombardi, became famous for his Green Bay sweep. That, too, was fundamental football, but not everyone can coach it.

"Jones' best play was off-tackle," Pappas said, "with two men blocking key men at the hole. The wingback and right end would block the tackle in, the blocking back and fullback would block the end out. Then, the two guards would pull. The first guard would get the linebacker and the next guard would get the defensive halfback. The left end would go down for the safety. He had a design to take care of almost everyone on the field."

Pappas recalled that Jones would painstakingly go through this play and others for hours in practice, demonstrating what he wanted done. And to get somebody's attention, he would take a stance and literally lower the boom on an unsuspecting Trojan lineman.

"Jones had an offensive theory," Pappas said. "First down, touchdown; second down, first down; third down, punt. He didn't use that fourth down for a punt until we got to our 40-yard line. Looking back, what was incredible was that we got most of our yardage on first and second downs."

Pappas said that rules discouraged passing during Jones' heyday because a pass had to be attempted five yards behind the line of scrimmage and a team couldn't throw two incomplete passes in one series. Otherwise, it would incur a five-yard penalty in both instances.

"You didn't pass as much as you wanted because there were so many penalties," Pappas said. "So you ran."

And run the Trojans did. Drury, a workhorse in the backfield, became USC's first 1,000-yard rusher (1,163) in 1927. Amazingly, the Trojans wouldn't have another 1,000-yard runner until Mike Garrett (1,440) in 1965.

Mort Kaer, USC's first All-American tailback, gained 852 yards in 1926; Saunders had 972 in 1929; Orv Mohler and Gus Shaver accounted for 983 and 936 in 1930 and 1931 and Cotton Warburton, an elusive, 145-pound runner, gained 885 yards in 1933.

All of these backs averaged better than five yards per carry with considerably fewer attempts (excepting Drury's 223 in 1927) than the modern-day USC tailback.

The records indicate that Jones must have been doing something right.

But the Headman did more than assemble powerful and almost unbeatable teams. He was loyal to his players, honest with the press and

Gus Shaver's 936 yards rushing in 1931 earned All-American honors and helped pace USC to its second national championship.

Orv Mohler averaged a spectacular 6.8 yards per carry in gaining 983 yards and All-American recognition in 1930.

Harry Smith anchored the line on Howard Jones' last great team, earning All-American honors in 1939.

Morley Drury, known more for his running, launches a pass in a season-opening 33-0 thumping of Occidental.

was a true sportsman who wouldn't tolerate foul play by his athletes.

An example of the lengths he would go to in order to make sure that his players played the game cleanly and fairly occurred in 1930.

USC and Stanford were involved in another important game and the Indians' chances of winning depended on the perfomance of Phil Moffat, a star halfback.

On the first play of the game, Moffat was hurt, leaving the field with a twisted knee. Jones immediately went to the Stanford locker room and asked Moffat if he knew which Trojan had hit him. Moffat replied that he did.

Jones asked, "Were you hit fairly?"

Moffat, dumbfounded at the question, could only stare at Jones.

An embarrassed Jones blurted out the question again: "What I mean . . . if you think . . . if it was a fair hit, it was all right and part of the game. But if your leg was deliberately twisted, the man who did it will never play another game for Southern California."

Moffat said that he had been tackled fairly. Jones said, "We don't want to win any other way on that field."

Jones was a private man and few knew him intimately. It was Wesson who best summed up the famous Trojan coach in a letter to the Los Angeles Times on the first anniversary of Jones' death:

"The Headman, because of a retiring nature, hated to make speeches. But he was a pigeon for a service club and never refused an invitation to talk at a meeting no matter how small and unimportant.

". . . He liked people who stood up straight and looked athletic. But he himself was always in a slouch and when standing in a group he always leaned on the guy nearest him.

"He never paid much attention to criticism heaped upon himself. But he burned and had plenty to say if anyone panned the game of football or any individual player.

"He demanded attention from his players when he talked. But when he was talked to, he never listened because he was always far away mentally wrestling with some football problem.

"He couldn't stand a guy who had had a drink. But he was the first to come to the aid of a confirmed rum pot who was helplessly under the influence.

"When Warner systems and Rockne systems and Model Ts began trying to hide the ball in the backfield, the Headman became more determined to rely principally on one ball-carrying ace, his quarterback. But he proved by his record that the best way to deceive the opposition was not to hide the ball from it but to knock them down.

"He told his boys that the game of football was fun principally for the battling hand-to-hand and rough-and-tumble contact in it. But, when he wanted fun, he invariably got the littlest, weakest fish in the high Sierras on his line.

"He was a perfect gentleman to strangers. But he never said a kind word to his closest friends. He would hardly glance at a boy coming off the field after playing his heart out.

But, when the game was over, in the privacy of the training quarters, he'd hunt out every boy who had played, thank him for what he had done, and be sure that any injuries, no matter how trivial, were immediately cared for.

"He didn't belong to a church. But he lived every minute of his life according to the Golden Rule."

And, many years later, Willis O. (Bill) Hunter, the USC athletic director when Jones was hired in 1925, said succinctly:

"I'd have to say that all of us hitched our wagon to a star, and Howard Jones was that star. He made all of USC's later success possible."

Cotton Warburton was one of USC's most exciting runners, earning All-American honors in 1933. Perhaps his most memorable play was a 60-yard jaunt against California. Almost every Cal player had a shot at the elusive Trojan. Amazingly, Warburton, who had been knocked unconscious earlier in the game, could remember nothing about the play.

Jack Clark, Cliff Propst, Nick Pappas and Jim Sutherland
kick up their heels in 1935. Pappas led the team in rushing
that year. He now serves USC as Associate Athletic
Director and Director of Athletic Funding.

John Ferraro, an All-American selection at tackle, helped the Trojans to an undefeated season in 1944, capped by a shutout victory over Tennessee in the Rose Bowl.

Chapter Four
THE WAITING PERIOD

It would not be precise to say that USC football was in limbo in the 40s and 50s. The Trojans went to the Rose Bowl five times during the time span and such players as Ralph Heywood, John Ferraro, Paul Cleary, Frank Gifford, Jim Sears, Jon Arnett and Marlin McKeever were honored as All-Americans.

There were also some fairly strong teams in this era — Jeff Cravath's war babies in the mid-40s and also his 1947 team, Jesse Hill's once-beaten 1952 team and Don Clark's 1959 club.

But the Trojans had established high standards under Howard Jones and alumni and fans of the school in the 40s and 50s thought in terms of national championships and took conference titles for granted.

Measured against the Thundering Herd days when overall only a loss or two in a season was tolerated, the 40s and 50s were a disappointing period for Trojan buffs. Sort of a waiting period.

The Trojans didn't win a national championship in this span and Notre Dame took charge of its series with USC. When Jones died, the Irish had only a slim edge over the Trojans — eight wins, six losses and a tie.

But Notre Dame had Frank Leahy in the 40s and part of the 50s — a coach of a Rockne or a Jones stature. As a result, the Irish beat the Trojans in 12 of 16 meetings with one tie.

Leahy's first victory over USC in 1941 wasn't indicative of what he would inflict on the Trojans in the future. The Irish won, 20-18, in a typically close competitive game.

But for USC, under its new head coach, Justin M. (Sam) Barry, it was just another loss in a season in which the Trojans won only two of nine games with one tie.

Barry had been a valued assistant for Jones. The Headman considered Barry to be his best scout and, when a defensive strategy stopped another team with the help of the information imparted by Barry, Jones always praised his assistant.

Barry had close ties with Jones. He became basketball and baseball coach at Iowa on Jones' recommendation. Later, Jones brought Barry to California to serve in the same capacity at USC in addition to his assistant football coaching duties.

Barry turned out winning baseball and basketball teams at USC and he was responsible for a major rules changes in the mid-30s — the abolition of the center jump. Moreover, his style of play, to some extent, was adopted by a famous basketball coach years later — California's Pete Newell.

Not only was Barry under football pressure

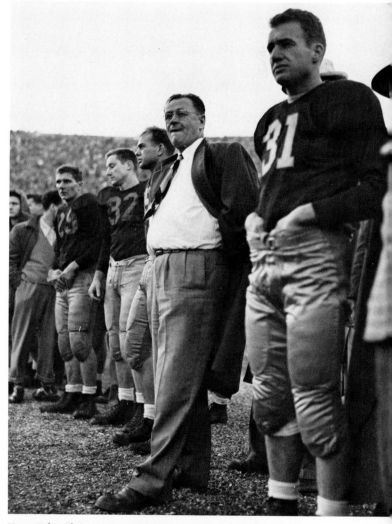

Newell (Jeff) Cravath, a defensive center on "Gloomy Gus" Henderson's 1924 Trojan squad, was named USC coach in 1942. During his career (he resigned in 1950), Cravath produced a respectable 54-28-8 record, highlighted by four Rose Bowl appearances.

in succeeding the legendary Jones, he wasn't left with much material. USC beat Oregon State, 13-7, in the 1941 opener (the Beavers would later play Duke in the transplanted Rose Bowl game at Durham), but won only one other game the rest of the season, a 7-6 squeaker over Washington State.

The bright spot in the season was the play of Bobby Robertson, a starting halfback under Jones as a sophomore in 1939. Robertson was a versatile back and accumulated 977 yards in total offense to lead the Pacific Coast Conference.

When the dismal season ended, it was rumored that Jock Sutherland, a famous Pittsburgh coach, would replace Barry. The rumor was denied by USC officials.

Barry, however, was called into military service and President Rufus B. von KleinSmid and athletic director Bill Hunter began looking for an interim coach. The choice was Newell (Jeff) Cravath, a former Jones' assistant and a hard-nosed defensive center for the Trojans from 1924 through 1926.

Cravath was coaching at the University of San Francisco in 1941 and his Dons had the highest scoring team on the West Coast. He had previously coached at Denver and in the junior college ranks.

A no-nonsense and sometimes hot-tempered coach on the field, but a warm-hearted man off-field, Cravath would later have problems dealing with his players.

He broke with the past and provided the Trojans with a new offensive look in 1942. Howard Jones' single wing, with the quarterback carrying the ball on almost every play, was put in mothballs.

The "T" formation, as popularized by Stanford's Rose Bowl team during the 1940 season, was in vogue and the Trojans were now in the "T" — with four backs, not one, handling the ball.

But USC had only moderate success in 1942, winning five and losing five with one tie. The Trojans lost to Tulane in the opener, 27-13, as a sophomore quarterback, Jim Hardy, rallied USC late in the game to avert a shutout.

The 1942 season is more memorable to UCLA fans because the Bruins beat the Trojans, 14-7, for the first time and earned that school's first bid to the Rose Bowl.

By 1943 the country's war effort was in full gear and, because of travel restrictions, teams

Ted Tannehill picks up yardage against Alabama in the 1946 Rose Bowl. Tannehill led the Trojans in rushing for the 1945 season.

Bob Robertson is finally dragged down after a 24-yard kickoff return against Washington State. Robertson was USC's leading rusher in 1940 and 1941.

generally played teams in their own area.

But USC football managed to flourish during the World War II years because Cravath was able to recruit on his own campus. Navy and Marine training programs were set up at the school and some athletes who had played at other schools were transferred to USC.

Moreover, the PCC voted to waive the peacetime regulation barring freshmen from varsity competition. So some beardless youngsters, such as 16-year-old end Jim Callanan and 17-year-old end-halfback Gordon Gray made valid contributions to the 1943 team.

Two other Callanans, Howard and George, both halfbacks, were already on the team, causing an identity problem for sportswriters.

USC played UCLA and California twice during each of the 1943, 1944 and 1945 seasons; Stanford dropped football during the war years. The Trojans improved on their series edge with the Bruins by winning five games with one tie.

USC also scheduled such service teams as St. Mary's Preflight, San Diego Navy and March Field which walloped the Trojans, 35-0, in 1943.

Cravath had an outstanding record during the war years, 23-6-2. His 1944 team was undefeated with two ties. USC made three straight appearances in the Rose Bowl.

In 1943 USC played Washington at Pasadena in the only matchup of West Coast teams in Rose Bowl history.

The Huskies were favored because they had beaten March Field, 27-7, during their abbreviated regular season. But the Trojans always seem at their best in the Rose Bowl. Hardy threw three touchdown passes to tie Russ Saunders' record as USC won easily, 29-0.

USC had an even better team in 1944. With Hardy leading the way with his play-calling and passing, the Trojans concluded an unbeaten season by defeating a young Tennessee team, 25-0, in the Rose Bowl. Callanan, now an 18-year-old veteran, scored the quickest touchdown in Rose Bowl history when he blocked a Tennessee punt and took it in with only 90 seconds elapsed in the game.

Because of service commitments, Hardy, All-American tackle John Ferraro, Gray and other stars from the 1944 team weren't available in 1945. So USC sent one of its worst teams to the Rose Bowl. The Trojans had a 7-3 regular season record, padded by the usual double victories over UCLA and California, but they weren't a strong team.

Alabama, led by quarterback Harry Gilmer, ended USC's string of eight Rose Bowl victories by winning, 34-14.

The war ended in 1945 and 1946 was the start of an unusual era in American college football. Servicemen who played for schools before the war, trainees who played during the war and incoming freshman all were competing for positions now.

Notre Dame and Michigan had some of their greatest teams in the post-World War II years. Likewise, USC and UCLA were loaded with talent, too.

But Cravath, some of his players said, had a disdain for the war veterans. He seemed to favor the players who played for him from 1943 through 1945. He worked his teams inordinately hard in 1946 and 1947 with tough, exhausting drills and scrimmages into the night.

Don Clark, who was a starting guard under

Does this number (32) and running style look familiar? Both were made famous twenty some years later by a man known simply as O.J. The "Juice's" forerunner here is Blake Headley in action during USC's 25-0 win over Tennessee in the 1945 Rose Bowl.

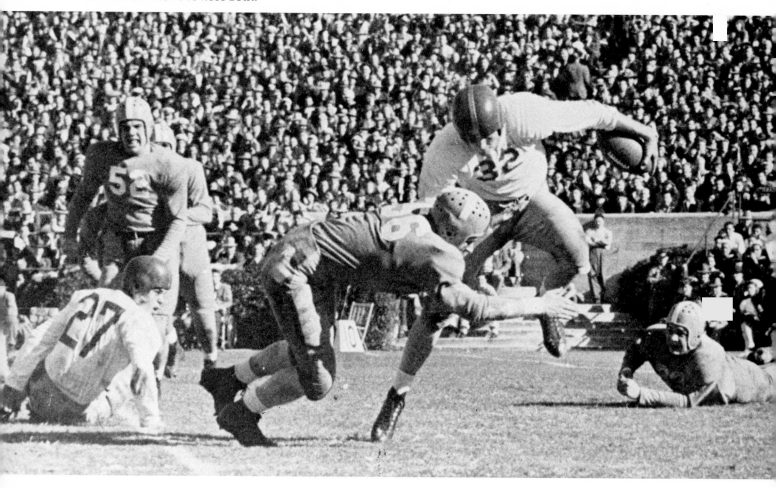

Cravath as a sophomore in 1942, spent 18 months in combat and won a battlefield commission. He told how it was for him to play for Cravath again.

"He was tough and firm when I played for him in 1942 but when I came back in 1946, he was an entirely different man," Clark said. "He seemed to have a complex about the service. Whether it was because he couldn't get into the service, I don't know.

"But, for whatever reason, he took it out on some of the servicemen. I seemed to be one of his pet peeves. He always made comments to me about the service, guts and things like that. And he seemed to favor those players who stayed around USC in the Navy's V-12 and V-5 programs, or those who weren't called into the service right away.

"And did we work. When he called a dummy scrimmage (supposedly no contact), you had to bring your brass knuckles. It was survival in those days, not of the fittest, but the luckiest."

Clark would become USC's football coach in 1957. Because of the arduous practice sessions he endured under Cravath, he said he tried to structure his own practices differently.

Cravath had perhaps too much talent on his postwar teams and because he couldn't play everyone, he had a lot of unhappy players.

USC had a disappointing 6-4 record in 1946 but in 1947 the Trojans took charge of the PCC again. After a 7-7 tie with Rice in the second game, USC began to roll. The Trojans beat Ohio State at Columbus, 32-0, and thrashed Oregon State, 48-6, to set up a climactic meeting with Pappy Waldorf's strong California team at Berkeley. Don Doll's 95-yard kickoff return to a touchdown at the start of the second half broke open a close game and USC went on to win impressively, 39-14.

But the Trojans had peaked too soon. They struggled thereafter even while winning, including a 6-0 victory over UCLA that clinched the Rose Bowl bid.

Then, Notre Dame, led by Johnny Lujack, Leon Hart, Emil Sitko, George Connor and company, destroyed USC, 38-7, before 104,953 fans — the largest crowd ever to see a game at the Coliseum, before or since.

The Trojans were humiliated again as Mighty Michigan dealt USC its worst defeat in the school's history, 49-0, in the 1948 Rose Bowl game.

The Trojans, according to Clark, scrimmaged up until nine o'clock the night before the Notre Dame game. Then, Cravath took 60 of his players to Santa Barbara before the Rose Bowl game and scrimmaged them relentlessly.

"We were a much better team than we showed against Notre Dame and Michigan," Clark recalled, "and we were dead tired before the Rose Bowl game because of the Santa Barbara sessions."

USC had respectable records of 6-3-1 in 1948, including an upset 14-14 tie with unbeaten Notre Dame, and 5-3-1 in 1949. When the Trojans slipped to 2-5-2 in 1950, one of the worst records in the school's history, Cravath was asked to resign. It was his only losing season and his overall record was a creditable 54-28-8 (.644), but dissatisfied alums reportedly pressured the administration to shelve Cravath.

Although he was unliked by some of his players, he was loved by others. Some say he wasn't cut out to be a head coach; others say he was treated unfairly, considering his record.

In any event, Cravath was out and USC didn't have to look far for its new coach: he was right on campus.

Jesse T. Hill had become USC's track coach when Dean Cromwell retired in 1949. Hill had been one of the school's best all-around athletes:

• He played fullback for Howard Jones in 1928-29. Although he never started a game, he had the highest rushing average in the Pacific Coast Conference, 8.2 yards a carry, his senior year.

• He picked up the nickname "Hula Hula" because of the manner in which he swerved his hips when he ran. Jones said he had never seen a faster man on Bovard Field.

• He lettered three years, 1927-1929, on the track team as a broad jumper, highlighting his USC career when he won the IC4A title with a leap of 25 feet, 7/8 of an inch, the first Trojan ever to better 25 feet in the event.

• He didn't report for baseball until his senior year at USC, but he was the leading hitter in the California Intercollegiate Baseball Association with a .389 average.

• He signed with the PCL Hollywood Stars at the end of the college schedule and, in his first time at bat, he hit a home run against the Los Angeles Angels at Wrigley Field.

• He played major league baseball for the

Jesse T. Hill held the USC coaching reins from 1951 through 1956, compiling a 45-17-1 record before moving up to the athletic director's post.

New York Yankees, Washington Senators and Oakland As and he retired with a 10-year batting average (majors and triple-A) of .306.

Like Gloomy Gus Henderson, Hill never achieved the acclaim as football coach that he probably deserved. He coached from 1951 through 1956 until he was promoted to athletic director and he had a 45-17-1 record, including two Rose Bowl appearances, a 7-0 win over Wisconsin in 1953 and a 20-7 loss to Ohio State in 1955. The win over Wisconsin was the first victory by a PCC team since the pact with the Big 10 had been conceived in 1947.

It was under Hill's regime that USC converted to a multiple offense, single wing and "T," to take advantage of the talents of Frank Gifford, who was a reserve "T" quarterback and defensive back under Cravath in 1949 and 1950.

Old Trojans still say it's a shame that Gifford was limited to only one season, his senior year in 1951, as a tailback. Otherwise, the versatile athlete who went on to become an All-Pro with

the New York Giants and then gain greater fame as a television sportscaster on ABC Monday Night Football would be mentioned in the same breath with O.J. Simpson and other famous USC tailbacks.

As it was, Gifford had an outstanding 1951 season, compiling 1,144 yards in total offense, 841 by rushing.

The Trojans finished with a 7-3 record, including a stirring 21-14 victory over California in which Gifford raced 69 yards for a touchdown with the Trojans trailing, 14-0.

It was the first regular season loss for Waldorf's Golden Bears since the 1947 season, or 38 consecutive games. It was in this game that USC's All-American linebacker Pat Cannamela was taunted by California rooters as being a "Dirty Trojan" for knocking Cal's famed back, Johnny Olszewski, out of the game with a hard tackle.

It was Hill's misfortune that his career coincided with that of UCLA's Henry (Red) Sanders, the Westwood school's most famous football coach.

UCLA had beaten USC only twice, in 1942 and in 1946, in a crosstown series that was inaugurated in 1929, but discontinued from 1931 through 1935, before Sanders arrived in 1949 from Vanderbilt.

Hill managed to beat Sanders only twice in his six years as USC's coach. One of the victories, 14-12 in 1952, was probably one of the most disappointing losses of the UCLA coach's career. For the first time in the history of the series, both teams were undefeated and untied going into the game. A possible national championship loomed as the prize for the winner.

The Trojans didn't go on to be accorded No. 1 status in the final wire service polls. Notre Dame spoiled what was otherwise a perfect USC season (10-1) by winning, 9-0. USC finished the year by beating Wisconsin in the Rose Bowl.

Hill had records of 6-3-1 in 1953, 8-4 in 1954, 6-4 in 1955 and 8-2 in 1956 before he replaced the retiring Bill Hunter as athletic director.

There were some outstanding USC players in the early 50s, including Gifford, Cannamela, Lindon Crow, Elmer Wilhoite, Jim Sears, an offensive threat who made All-American in 1952 as a defensive back, Al Carmichael, Bob Van Doren, Leon Clarke, Lou Welsh, George Timberlake, Aramis Dandoy, C.R. Roberts,

In his first season as coach (1951), Jess Hill made one of his smartest moves ever. He moved a poorly utilized defensive back and quarterback named Frank Gifford into the tailback slot in USC's newly implemented multiple offense. The season saw Gifford gather All-American honors while amassing over 1,100 yards in total offense. It also launched a career that still has Gifford as one of the most recognized personalities in the world of sports.

Marv Goux — and Jon Arnett.

Arnett was one of the most exciting runners ever to play for USC. An accomplished gymnast and broad jumper at Manual Arts High near USC, he did things seldom seen on a football field.

He would take a clean hit and be propelled into the air; then, like a cat, would land in a crouch and take off again. Arnett was USC's leading rusher in 1954 and 1955 with 601 and 672 yards on a total of only 237 carries.

Arnett played only half a season in 1956 as a senior because of PCC penalties levied against athletes from USC, UCLA, California and Washington for taking under-the-table payments in excess of what the conference allowed for living expenses.

Other players who were juniors in 1956 lost their eligibility for the 1957 season. C.R. Roberts, an explosive fullback, who teamed with Arnett to beat Notre Dame, 42-20, in 1955 and rushed for a then-school record of 251 yards against Texas in 1956, was one of the players affected.

The scandals not only scarred the players but led to the dissolution of the Pacific Coast Conference in 1959. A new league, the Athletic Association of Western Universities (AAWU) was formed with USC, UCLA, California, Washington and later Stanford as the member schools. It wouldn't be until 1964 that all of the Northwest schools would become reunited with the Big Five in the Pacific 8, which is now the Pac-10.

It was hardly a time for a new coach to take over at USC. But Don Clark, captain of the 1947 Trojans, a star lineman with the San Francisco 49ers and an assistant under Hill, was persuaded to take the job.

"When I became coach, we hadn't recruited for two years," Clark said. "They (the PCC) didn't say we couldn't recruit but they put severe restrictions on us. In the spring of 1957, we were down to walk-ons — no quarterbacks or receivers to speak of."

It is understandable why the Trojans had their worst record, 1-9, in the school's history in 1957, beating only Washington.

Al Carmichael heads upfield against Wisconsin in the 1953 Rose Bowl. Carmichael scored the game's only touchdown on a pass from Rudy Bukich for a 7-0 USC victory.

PHOTO COURTESY OF PASADENA TOURNAMENT OF ROSES ASSOCIATION

What Frank Gifford was to USC's offense in 1951, Pat Cannamela was to the defense. Both were All-Americans in 1951 and both had perhaps their greatest moments in the Trojan's 21-14 comeback win over California. It was the Golden Bears' first regular season defeat since 1947, a 38-game streak.

C. R. Roberts rambles for 22 yards with a screen pass against Notre Dame in 1955. Roberts was a strong, versatile fullback who teamed with Jon Arnett to give the Trojans yet another strong running attack in the mid-1950's. They were at their best in this 42-20 victory over the Paul Hornung-led Fighting Irish. Roberts' most outstanding individual performance was against Texas the next year when he rushed for 251 yards in only twelve minutes of playing time, leading USC to a 44-20 win.

Clark tried to generate enthusiasm with snappy workouts and a new "go-go-go" system, a hurry-up offense that was implemented by him along with assistant coach Al Davis. This was the same Al Davis who is credited by some later with forcing the merger of the NFL and AFL. He is now the eminently successful owner of the Oakland Raiders.

Clark was an organized man and he didn't become discouraged. When he was able to recruit again — getting players like the McKeever twins, Mike and Marlin — the Trojans made a comeback. They were 4-5-1 in 1958 and 8-2 in 1959, losing to UCLA and Notre Dame in the last two games.

Then Clark walked away from the job.

"I had never planned on staying in athletics," he said. "I just took the USC job to help build the program back up."

And build it he did after becoming coach in 1957 at a time when USC had lost 19 lettermen from the 1956 team — 11 by graduation and eight by ineligibility because of the PCC penalties.

Clark went out as a winner and applied the same success formula to the family business — Prudential Overall Supply, which has grown to 10 plants with approximately 700 employees.

So USC was without a coach on the threshold of the 60s. The most ardent Trojan fan couldn't imagine that the next coach would elevate the school to the national prominence that had not been attained since the days of Howard Jones.

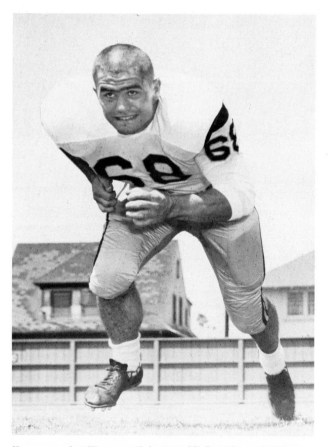

How many families can claim two All-Americans in the same year? Marlin (86) at end and Mike McKeever (68) at linebacker both made the honor roll as they helped USC to an 8-2 record in 1959, the best year for coach Don Clark. Marlin repeated the next season.

Following a miserable 1-9 record in 1957 (their worst
ever) and a lackluster 4-5-1 in 1958, the Trojans bounced
back with a record of eight wins against two losses in
1959. Much of the credit can be given to the senior
leadership provided by defensive specialists Ron Mix
(left) and Willie Wood.

John McKay personified USC football for 16 seasons. He is thought by many to have had more influence on offensive college football than any coaching contemporary, largely because of his development of the "I" formation. Yet, conference in every critical defensive category. McKay left USC following the 1975 season with four national championships, 127 victories and a ticket to the professional coaching ranks in his pocket.

Chapter Five
"I" FOR "INNOVATIVE"

Intelligent. Witty. Flippant. Quick-tempered. Moody. Aloof. Charming. Introverted.

John McKay is all of these things — and more. To those who knew him best, the former USC coach, now coaching Tampa Bay of the NFL, was and is an enigma.

But his friends and detractors generally agree that he'll be remembered as one of the outstanding college coaches of all time.

Not only did he restore USC to its elite status which the school has maintained today under John Robinson, but he also probably had more influence on the way offensive football is played at the college level than any other coach in his time.

It was McKay who modernized the "I" formation with the tailback standing up in the backfield some seven yards deep, with the vision to scan the defense and with the potential to strike at almost any point along the line.

When you talk about tailbacks, you're talking about USC — such glamour runners as Mike Garrett and O.J. Simpson, both Heisman Trophy winners; Clarence Davis, Anthony Davis and Ricky Bell — all from the McKay era — and Charles White, the latest Heisman winner.

McKay was innovative, but more important than that, he was a winner. He won four national championships (1962, 1967, 1972, 1974) during his 16 years at USC (1960-75). His teams won nine Pacific 8 titles and finished in the nation's top 10 in the final wire service polls on nine occasions. He had a career record of 127-40-8 (.749), putting him in the same class with the legendary Howard Jones (.750). McKay's teams played a far more ranging and difficult schedule than the USC teams of the 20s and 30s.

The Rose Bowl became almost USC's second home during McKay's tenure. His teams made eight New Year's Day appearances in Pasadena, winning five and losing three.

There was an exciting quality about McKay's teams and some of the most memorable games in USC history were played in the 60s and 70s:

The 42-37 victory over Wisconsin in the 1963 Rose Bowl game.

The 20-17 win over Notre Dame in 1964, the game that deprived the Irish of the national championship.

The 21-20 squeaker over UCLA in 1967 with Simpson sprinting 64 yards for the clinching touchdown.

A final-minutes 14-12 conquest of the Bruins in 1969, over Stanford 26-24, and again in 1973, 27-26.

The amazing 55-24 rout of Notre Dame in 1974 after the Trojans trailed, 24-6, at halftime.

The late, 18-17 victory over Ohio State in the

Bill Nelsen (26), shown challenging Pittsburgh defenders in 1961, led the Trojans in total offense for the 1960 and 1961 seasons.

1975 Rose Bowl game.

USC is identified with its tailbacks but rival coaches say it was the strength and mobility of McKay's offensive lines that enabled Simpson & Company to run to daylight.

On any NFL roster there probably was or is a Trojan lineman: Ron Yary and Steve Riley of Minnesota, Gerry Mullins of Pittsburgh, Bob Klein of San Diego, John Grant of Denver, Marvin Powell of the New York Jets, Gary Jeter of the New York Giants, John Vella of Oakland are but a sampling.

USC had more than its share of All-Americans and talented players during the McKay era: wide receivers Hal Bedsole, Lynn Swann and Bobby Chandler; tight end Charles Young; linebackers Damon Bame, Adrian Young, Charley Weaver, Jimmy Gunn, Willie Hall and Richard Wood; defensive end Tim Rossovich; offensive tackles Sid Smith and

McKay and the Trojans congratulate fullback Ben Wilson during USC's 25-0 victory over the Fighting Irish. This contest capped an undefeated season. assured a national championship and set the stage for a 1963 Rose Bowl appearance against Wisconsin.

Pete Adams; defensive backs Mike Battle, Artimus Parker and Marvin Cobb; quarterbacks Mike Rae, Jimmy Jones and Pat Haden and fullbacks Sam (Bam) Cunningham and Ben Wilson.

During the 40s and 50s, the USC-Notre Dame series had become one-sided, distinctly favoring the Irish. But McKay, after a tentative start against Notre Dame, turned things around.

He was shut out by the Irish his first two seasons, 1960 and 1961, and in 1966 Notre Dame embarrassed USC, 51-0, the worst defeat in Trojan history.

Although McKay denies the story which may be apocryphal, he reportedly said after that game that Notre Dame will never beat me again (or, perhaps, as badly).

In any event, McKay lost only *once* to Notre Dame the next nine seasons (two ties). When he left USC for Tampa Bay after the 1975 season, he had established an 8-6-2 record against the Irish.

McKay is a stocky man, 5-feet-9-inches and the weight varies, of Scotch-Irish descent. He grew up in the coal-mining country of West Virginia and excelled in football and basketball at Shinnston High School.

He had ambitions even then to become a coach. After serving as a tailgunner on a B-29 in World War II, where he learned to meditate and smoke cigars, he enrolled at Purdue. He played freshman football there in 1946, then transferred to Oregon the next year.

McKay was an All-Coast halfback at Oregon, teaming in the backfield with his friend, Norm Van Brocklin, who later became a famous pro quarterback with the Rams and Eagles.

McKay stayed on as an assistant at Oregon, where he was valued for his offensive input, recruiting and scouting. Nick Pappas, USC's associate athletic director and a former assistant football coach, still marvels to this day about the way McKay scouted a game.

"He never took notes, while the rest of us were scribbling furiously," Pappas said. "Yet he knew everything that was going on and would occasionally lean over and tell me that this player should be in this spot and so on."

McKay, in his book, *A Coach's Story,* written with Jim Perry, USC's sports information director, minimizes his skill as a superscout.

"I wasn't a genius. I just had a simpler method than the other scouts," McKay said. "I believed that teams at that time had a

ARNOLD FRANKEL

Two of college football's living legends — Paul "Bear" Bryant of Alabama and John McKay. Between them these men have collected ten national championships. Bryant, of course, is still in the hunt for more.

67

Pete Beathard (12) makes this leaping interception and USC goes on to upend the 1962 Duke Blue Devils. Beathard was an outstanding athlete, able to play both ways which was still a requirement in the waning years of limited substitutions.

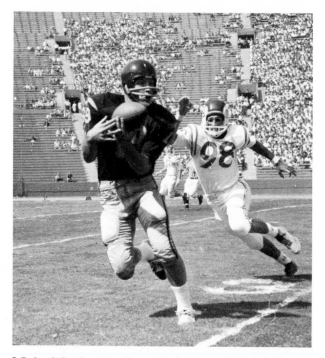

A Duke defender watches as All-American Hal Bedsole gathers the pigskin and heads toward the end zone. At 6-feet-5-inches, 220 pounds, Bedsole was uncommonly big for a wide receiver. Bedsole holds the USC single season record for touchdown receptions with 11.

defense they wanted to play, and they would use it perhaps 85 percent of the time. For example, Red Sanders' UCLA teams in the mid-50s played with what we called a 4-4, or wide-six defense. I'd watch all the other scouts draw a diagram every time UCLA lined up, putting down the entire Bruin defense.

"I thought this was ridiculous. I knew where UCLA was lining up 85 percent of the time. So, unless they lined up differently, all I had to say to myself or write was '60'. I watched UCLA and it was 60, 60, 60. I could then see the game while the other scouts were laboriously writing. There's no way you can draw 11 diagrams, write 11 names and watch the whole play. But this is one of the things that (head) coaches wanted. It was stupid.

"So other scouts would miss a man or two and ask me what defense they were in and I'd say brightly, 'They were in 60. This guy was here and that guy was there.' And they'd think I was a genius."

Pappas was so impressed by McKay's ability to reduce what is considered a complex game to simple terms that when an opening developed on Don Clark's staff in 1959, he implored Clark to hire McKay.

McKay agonized over the decision, but finally accepted. His wife, the former Corky Hunter who grew up in Southern California, helped persuade him to take the USC job.

It was the most fortuitous decision of McKay's career. Clark resigned after the 1959 season, among other reasons, to help his brother run the family business.

Clark recommended McKay for the USC job. After he was formally offered the position by USC president Norman Topping, McKay recalled that it took him a half a second to say yes.

Now USC football was in the hands of a virtually unknown assistant coach and his debut was hardly auspicious. He lost his 1960 opener to Oregon State, 14-0, and struggled through a 4-6 season.

Injuries, graduation losses and an inordinate number of slow-footed backs hindered the Trojans. Alumni were already grumbling about McKay when the new USC coach upset UCLA, 17-6, near the end of the season. "It was an important game," McKay said later. "It only saved my job."

He fashioned that upset with defensive strategy. McKay is renowned as an offensive coach, but he is also a sound defensive strategist and his stronger teams in later years would always lead the Pacific 8 in every meaningful defensive category.

"I can't say enough about the importance of defense," McKay once said. "Coaches without a good defense don't sleep at night. With a good one, there's always a chance for victory. With a poor one, there's always a great chance for defeat. If we have a super offense sitting on the bench all day, it does us no good at all."

The record was not much better in 1961, 4-5-1, but McKay was already experimenting with the "I" formation. He moved Willie Brown, a flanker, to tailback, and Brown responded with a 93-yard touchdown run to beat SMU.

Then, the following week in a nationally televised game against Iowa, USC had its first explosive offensive game under McKay. After trailing, 21-0, the Trojans rallied for 34 points. They lost in the final minute, 35-34, when

Damon Bame (64), typifying McKay's defensive philosophy, interrupts the passing plans of Illinois quarterback Ron Fearn.

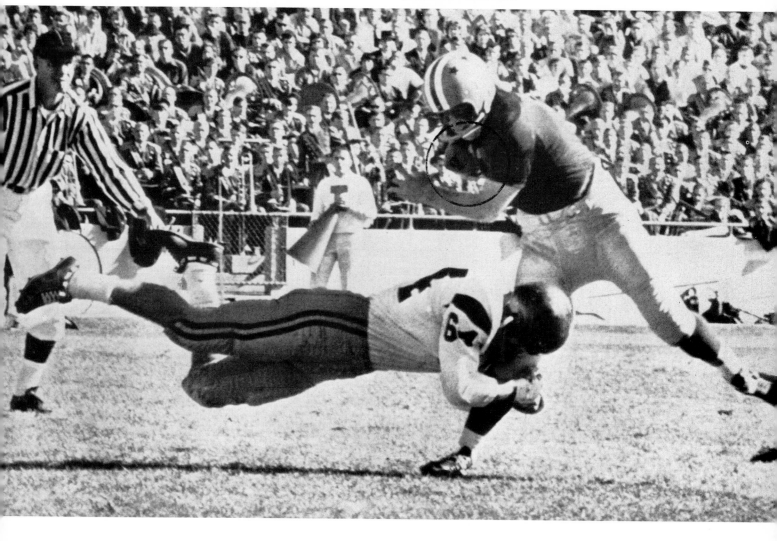

Ben Wilson (49) dives over Notre Dame's defense for the
first touchdown in the Trojans' thrashing of the Irish in
1962. The victory sewed up the national championship and
USC's first perfect season since 1932.

Willie Brown became USC's first "I" tailback in 1962,
although he was so versatile he was often used as a split
end or flanker. He shows the position's potential going
through a gaping hole against Wisconsin in the 1963 Rose
Bowl.

McKay, not willing to settle for a tie with a one-point conversion try, opted for the two-pointer and failed. He would lose other games by electing to go for two points, but he would also win a Rose Bowl game and a share of the national championship with a successful two-point try. McKay saw no sense in ties; he played only to win.

In 1962 it all came together for McKay. He had benefited from recruiting, refined the "I" and borrowed the Arkansas defense from Frank Broyles.

USC had speed on both offense and defense, two fine quarterbacks in Pete Beathard and Bill Nelsen, the versatile Willie Brown at tailback, strong Ben Wilson at fullback and wide receiver Hal Bedsole, a big man (6-5, 220), who could fly with his feet on the ground.

The 1962 team not only had a perfect 11-0 record to win the national championship. In its 10 regular season games, USC out-scored the opposition, 219-55, and held eight opponents to seven points or less.

Highlights of the season included a 14-0 victory over Washington, the dominant team on the West Coast since 1959; a hard-earned 14-3 win over UCLA in which Brown made an incredible stretching catch to set up a touchdown and a 25-0 victory over Notre Dame that clinched the national championship.

But the best and most thrilling aspect of the season was yet to come — the 1963 Rose Bowl game with Wisconsin. The Trojans built what seemed an almost insurmountable lead, 42-14, on Beathard's passing. They almost lost the game when Wisconsin quarterback Ron VanderKelen completed 18 of 22 passes in the fourth quarter, 33 of 48 in the game for 401 yards, in a remarkable near-comeback. Final score: USC 42, Wisconsin 37.

The 1963 season is notable for the debut of the first of McKay's great tailbacks — chunky,

Heisman Trophy winner Mike Garrett is honored by USC president Dr. Norman Topping (at microphone) and athletic director Jess Hill (center) in an emotional ceremony after his last game against Wyoming in 1965.

5-foot-9-inch, 185-pound Mike Garrett, a runner with speed and power.

McKay said it's a shame that Garrett never got an opportunity to play in the Rose Bowl during his three seasons at USC. The Trojans had respectable records — 7-3 in 1963 and again in 1964 and 7-2-1 in 1965 — but losses to Washington and UCLA kept them from returning to Pasadena.

One of the most disheartening losses of McKay's career came in 1965 against the Tommy Prothro-coached UCLA team.

The Trojans dominated the Bruins most of the game and led, 16-6, at one time. Garrett wound up with 210 yards on 40 carries. But Gary Beban's late-scoring bomb to Kurt Altenberg provided UCLA with the Rose Bowl bid, 20-16.

USC just missed getting to the Rose Bowl in the mid-60s, but there was that shining moment in 1964 when the Trojans shocked Notre Dame right out of a national championship.

The unbeaten Irish were on their way to a national title, leading the Trojans, 17-0, at halftime. But the Trojans rallied to win, 20-17, on quarterback Craig Fertig's touchdown pass

Tim Rossovich (88), an All-American at defensive end, kicks one of eight extra points (a USC record) against Wyoming in 1965.

to wide receiver Rod Sherman. Many Trojan fans consider this to be *the* classic game in a classic series.

USC got to the Rose Bowl in 1966, but McKay doesn't have pleasant memories of that season. The Trojans lost their final three games — UCLA, 14-7; Notre Dame 51-0, and Purdue in the Rose Bowl, 14-13, when McKay lost another two-point gamble.

The Bruins were outraged that they weren't invited to the Rose Bowl, arguing that their 9-1 record and upset win over USC were credentials enough. But Pacific 8 teams did not play a round-robin schedule then, and USC ostensibly got the bid on the basis of a better conference record than UCLA — 4-1 to 3-1.

The 1966 season was a downer for USC because of the way it collapsed at the end. The next year, however, became significant for two reasons: one, a junior college transfer from San Francisco named Orenthal James Simpson was the new tailback. Two, the Trojans were on their way to three winning years in which they would have a combined 29-2-2 record, win the national championship and finish second and third in wire service rankings and make three straight visits to the Rose Bowl.

When USC won its first national title under McKay in 1962, it was accomplished under one-platoon rules. In 1967 the two-platoon system was back and McKay had an even stronger team.

The incomparable Simpson averaged 154 yards a game rushing, including a single game high of 235 yards.

McKay had one of his best defensive units which allowed only 87 points in 11 games.

And 1967 was the year of the team that broke the South Bend jinx. Notre Dame hadn't lost to USC at home since 1939 but Simpson's running and a ball-hawking defense that included seven interceptions retired some old ghosts, 24-7.

There was also the showdown game with crosstown rival UCLA. The Bruins were the nation's top-ranked team at the time. The Trojans had held the No. 1 position earlier, but had slipped to third the previous week after being upset by Oregon State, 3-0, on a muddy field at Corvallis.

From the standpoint of significance, excitement and the unexpected, USC's series with Notre Dame is rivaled only by its annual meetings with UCLA.

The 1967 game was something special. The

Ron Yary, a 1967 and 1968 All-American at offensive tackle, remains USC's only Outland Trophy winner.

All-American linebacker Adrian Young holds the USC record for single game interceptions with four against Notre Dame in 1967.

lead changed hands four times. UCLA spurted ahead, 20-14, in the fourth quarter behind Gary Beban, the Heisman Trophy-winning quarterback. Then, Simpson found daylight and sprinted 64 yards to a touchdown and a national championship.

After that, even the Rose Bowl was anticlimactic. Indiana, making its first trip to Pasadena, was dominated by USC, 14-3.

The next two years the Trojans got another nickname — the Cardiac Kids; the team won or tied 12 times with fourth-quarter comebacks.

In 1968 McKay had only 15 lettermen to augment O.J. who virtually *was* the USC offense, although Steve Sogge, a heady quarterback, threw enough to prevent defenses from keying on the famous tailback.

Simpson carried the ball 383 times, an average of 35 carries a game, and gained 1,880 yards, an average of 4.9 yards a carry, on his way to winning the Heisman Trophy.

Some reporters implied that McKay was overworking Simpson. The USC coach, in what has now become a much-repeated quote, quipped:

"The ball isn't heavy. Anyway, O.J. doesn't belong to a union."

USC came from behind to beat Stanford and Oregon State and broke ties in the last five minutes to defeat Washington and Oregon. The Trojans were ranked No. 1 in the latter part of the season until they had to rally to tie Notre Dame, 21-21. They slipped to No. 2.

USC came into the Rose Bowl against Ohio State with a 9-0-1 record. Despite an 80-yard touchdown run by Simpson, the Buckeyes took advantage of Trojan turnovers to win, 27-16.

The 1969 team had a 10-0-1 record, climaxing the season with a 10-3 victory over Michigan in the Rose Bowl. But the second edition of the Cardiac Kids was often maligned because they didn't win by impressive margins.

The fabulous Juice was gone and the Trojans had a new personality — a team that was led by

Rarely have talent, personality and character been mixed as well as they have been in the personage of O.J. Simpson. The result is one of the true superstars. These pictures should be of particular interest to defensive linemen, most of whom only saw the "Juice" as a passing blur.

Along with world-class speed, O.J. had the size (6-feet-2-inches, 207 pounds) and power to run inside when necessary as he shows against Washington and UCLA.

sophomore quarterback Jimmy Jones, tailback Clarence Davis and an active defensive line known as the Wild Bunch.

Jones was a quarterback who could misfire on eight straight passes and then become accurate in the final minutes.

Davis is now known as the "forgotten" USC tailback because his career followed those of Garrett and Simpson. Davis led the Trojans in rushing in 1969 and 1970, gaining 1,351 and 972 yards, and later became a valued running back for the Oakland Raiders.

The name, Wild Bunch, was inspired by the movie of the same name. The group was composed of ends Jimmy Gunn and Charles Weaver, tackles Al Cowlings and Tody Smith and middle guard Bubba Scott. Gunn and Cowlings were All-Americans in 1969. Weaver was so honored in 1970.

The Cardiac Kids were at their heart-stopping best in a 26-24 victory over Stanford. Stanford quarterback Jim Plunkett had apparently beaten the Trojans, 24-23, with a long pass that preceded a field goal late in the game. USC surged back behind Jones' passing and Davis' running to set up Ron Ayala's 34-yard field goal with no time remaining.

The 1969 USC-UCLA game is considered

Steve Sogge (9), quarterback of the Trojans in 1967 and 1968, turns upfield to find yardage.

one of the most dramatic of the series. Both teams were unbeaten with 8-0-1 records, but USC could clinch a Rose Bowl berth with a tie because the Bruins' league record was marred by a tie and the Trojans had a perfect conference mark.

The Wild Bunch gave UCLA quarterback Dennis Dummit a fearful beating, but the Trojans couldn't make much headway against the Bruins. USC led 7-6 most of the game, but UCLA took the lead, 12-7, on Dummit's short touchdown pass with five minutes left.

Then, Jones, 0 for 9 passing in the first half, began to hit his receivers. A pass interference penalty against UCLA on an apparent fourth-down incompletion game Jones a reprieve. The quarterback fired a 32-yard touchdown pass to Sam Dickerson deep in the end zone — and

Mike Battle (17) is shown here in action against UCLA. The All-American defensive back is one of only two Trojans to have gained over 1,000 career yards returning punts. Three of Battle's returns ended in touchdowns, a USC record.

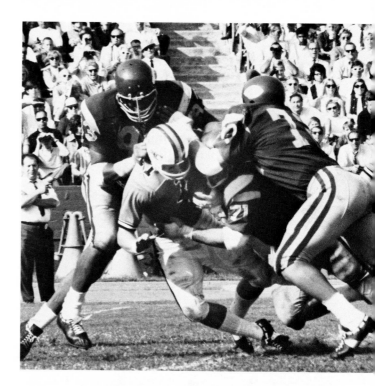

An awesome defensive line (tagged "The Wild Bunch") helped the Trojans to a 10-0-1 record in 1969. Pictured in these photographs during the 1969 Georgia Tech game are examples of Wild Bunch "handiwork" by such stalwarts as Tody Smith (93), Willard (Bubba) Scott (71), Carl Nielsen (73) and Charlie Weaver (84).

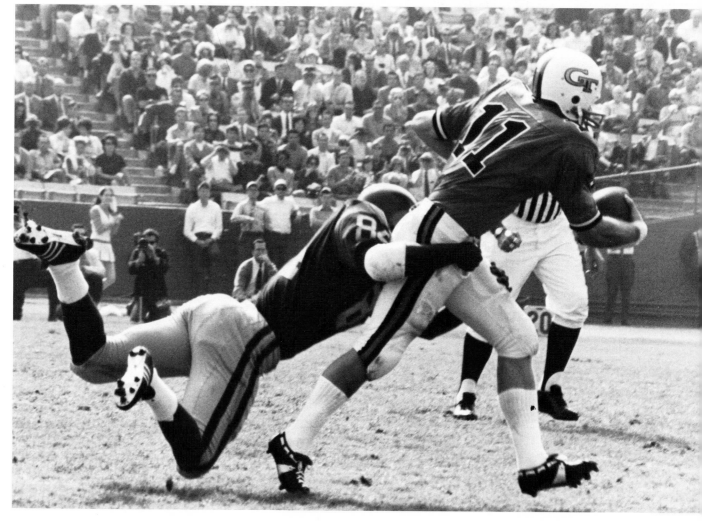

USC had pulled it out, 14-12, with 1:32 to play.

McKay was now at the peak of his profession. His teams contended for the national championship every year, they played exciting, interesting football and they were appreciated by nonpartisans who watched them on television.

It appeared that the winning beat would go on and on. USC opened the 1970 season with four wins including an impressive 42-21 rout of Alabama at Birmingham, and a 21-21 tie with Nebraska.

Then USC lost to Plunkett-led Stanford, 24-14, and the Trojan Horse threw a shoe. USC lost three of its remaining six games, including a demoralizing 45-20 setback to UCLA. A pattern was developing.

USC was 6-4-1 in 1970 and matched that in 1971. Winning years in some books, but not at USC. The years were viewed as mediocre at best because of the high standards set earlier by McKay.

There were some "ups" in those "down" years. USC still managed to upset Notre Dame, winning 38-28 in 1970 and 28-14 in 1971 at South Bend.

McKay did some soul-searching and came to the realization that he and his staff had unwittingly become complacent in recruiting. They settled sometimes for marginal players instead of the best. His teams also lacked speed. With more and more teams going to the triple-option offense, quick, fast players, especially on defense, were essential.

McKay became speed conscious and the Trojans haven't really been slow since. The

Bob Klein had an outstanding career at tight end for the Trojans and went on to make quite a name for himself in the pros.

All-American tailback Clarence Davis (28), shown here against UCLA in 1969, gains several of his 1,351 yards of the season.

USC image is that of a big, physically overpowering team, generally a true reflection of the Trojans' pro-sized offensive lines. But McKay and his successor often look to the smaller, more agile players on defense.

McKay became conscious in 1970 that he needed faster and more talented players. By 1972 he had the right blend of experience and youth. He also had one of the greatest teams in the history of college football.

This was a team without an apparent weakness. It had a 12-0 record, scored 467 points, averaged 432 yards a game, never trailed in the second half, restricted opponents to an average of only 2.5 yards per rush and didn't permit a run longer than 29 yards.

McKay had two quality quarterbacks, senior Mike Rae and sophomore Pat Haden; an outstanding sophomore tailback, Anthony Davis, who became a starter at midseason; a high diving, excellent blocking fullback, Sam (Bam) Cunningham; tight end Charles Young and offensive tackle Pete Adams, both All-Americans; skilled defensive players like tackles John Grant and Jeff Winans and Richard (Batman) Wood, a sophomore All-American linebacker who could run the 40 in 4.5 seconds, and three fine wide receivers, Lynn Swann, Edesel Garrison and Johnny McKay, the coach's son.

USC met fourth-ranked Arkansas, a team with national championship aspirations, in the opener at Little Rock. USC won, 31-10, and never looked back the rest of the season.

Defensive end Jimmy Gunn pursues a Notre Dame ball carrier during the 1968 confrontation in the Coliseum. Chase scenes such as this led to All-American status in 1969, when Gunn served as a card-carrying member of "The Wild Bunch."

In one of the most dramatic games in the USC-UCLA series in 1969, Jimmy Jones came back from a horrible 0-for-9 first-half passing to hit Sam Dickerson with a 32-yard touchdown pass with 1:32 left to win, 14-12.

The Wild Bunch kept the pressure on UCLA's Dennis Dummit all day, enabling the Trojans to stay close to the Bruins in the 1969 classic until Jones and Dickerson's heroics could pull the game out.

The Trojans got 50 or more points in routing Oregon State, Illinois and Michigan State. They breezed through the rest of their schedule including a 24-7 victory over UCLA, which had a ground-consuming, wishbone offense — until it met USC.

The regular-season ending game was with Notre Dame at the Coliseum. The Irish made a game of it, and closed to within two points of the lead, 25-23, late in the third quarter.

Then Anthony Davis returned a kickoff 96 yards for a touchdown. He had earlier scored on a 97-yard kickoff return. The momentum belonged to the Trojans and they won, 45-23.

Davis scored *six* touchdowns against Notre Dame, the most ever by a Trojan running back. A unique headline in the Los Angeles Times said it all the next day: Davis, Davis, Davis, Davis, Davis, Davis!

The 5-foot-9-inch, 175-pound tailback, who strutted like a drum major when he ran, went on to become an All-American, but he never had such a rewarding afternoon again.

To underscore that the team was clearly the best in the country, USC destroyed Woody Hayes' Ohio State team, 42-17, in the Rose Bowl. Cunningham sky-dived for four touchdowns, Rae completed 18 of 25 passes for 229 yards with no interceptions and Davis slashed for 157 yards, including a 20-yard touchdown run that broke the game open.

The Trojans were undisputed as No. 1. For the first time in history, USC got every first-place ballot in the final AP and UPI polls.

McKay had lost 12 regulars from his 1972 team when the 1973 season opened. Still, the Trojans responded with a 9-2-1 record and another appearance in the Rose Bowl.

USC started fast with a 6-0 record and a No. 1 national ranking. Notre Dame, smarting from the defeats McKay had inflicted for three straight years, got a measure of revenge. The Irish beat the Trojans, 23-14, at South Bend, ending USC's 23-game unbeaten streak.

The Trojans rebounded to beat Stanford, 27-26, on Chris Limahelu's 34-yard field goal with three seconds left and they defeated a favored UCLA, 23-13. The Bruins, running

George Yablonsky, head equipment manager at USC since 1967, sizes up Trojan split end Sam Dickerson.

out of Pepper Rodgers' wishbone, had averaged 49 points and 415 yards rushing a game.

McKay showed his flair for defense again as he shut down UCLA's talented running backs, James McAlister and Kermit Johnson; relied on a ball control offense that featured a key touchdown pass from Haden to Johnny McKay and won, 23-13.

The win sent USC to the Rose Bowl for another match with Ohio State. Hayes' Buckeyes were considered stronger than his 1968 national championship team. USC was in the game most of the way, leading at one time, 21-20. But Ohio State prevailed, 42-21. Haden completed 21 of 39 passes for 229 yards, but his receivers, including the usually reliable Swann, dropped pass after pass.

McKay had reason to believe that he had one of the strongest teams in the country at the outset of the 1974 season. Haden and Davis

Jimmy Jones, Clarence Davis (28) and the rest of the Trojans concluded a great 10-0-1 season in 1969 with a solid 10-3 win over Michigan in the Rose Bowl.

were both seniors. The team was generally experienced.

The Trojans were shocked by Arkansas, 22-7, in the opener at Little Rock, prompting the Los Angeles Times headline: USC's Dreams of No. 1 All Hogwash.

The Trojans weren't impressive at times, especially at mid-season when they were tied by California, 15-15. But then they got rolling. In order, USC whipped Stanford, 34-10; Washington, 42-11 and UCLA, 34-9.

Then came one of the most remarkable games ever played. The Trojans, apparently beaten by Notre Dame and trailing, 24-0, in the first half, rallied for 35 points in the third quarter, scored some more in the fourth quarter and won, 55-24.

Anthony Davis returned the second-half kickoff 102 yards for a touchdown to get the roll started — frustrating Notre Dame coach Ara Parseghian again. Davis' long kickoff

Charlie Weaver, a member of the Wild Bunch in 1969, earned 1970 All-American honors as a defensive end for plays like this.

return was the sixth of his career, breaking the existing NCAA record.

The Trojans, with a flair for the dramatic, had not run out of comebacks. In the 1975 Rose Bowl game, USC trailed Ohio State, 17-10, with minutes left to play. Haden teamed with Johnny McKay, his favorite receiver when both played at Bishop Amat High School, on a 38-yard touchdown pass. Coach McKay went for the two-point conversion try. This time his dice came up "seven" as Haden threw a low, accurate pass to Shelton Diggs in the end zone for an 18-17 victory. The pass was the biggest play of the year because Alabama had

lost to Notre Dame on New Year's night in the Orange Bowl and USC was elevated to the No. 1 spot in the final UPI poll.

Eight starters from the 1974 team were available in 1975. McKay had lost such proven players as Haden, Davis, Johnny McKay, lineman Art Riley, linebacker Dale Mitchell and defensive backs Marvin Cobb and Charles Phillips.

USC, however, didn't elicit any sympathy from its Pacific 8 rivals who propagandized that the Trojans were "always loaded." The propaganda seemed to be the truth as USC won its first seven games, including a 24-17 victory

Seven times linebackers in the McKay era were named All-Americans. This one is Willie Hall, in action against California in 1971.

Rarely has a player been able to switch positions in mid-career. John Vella is one of the exceptions. A defensive lineman in 1970 (above), Vella became an All-American at offensive tackle in 1971.

86

over Notre Dame at South Bend. Ricky Bell, a converted fullback-linebacker, was the new Trojan tailback and he gained 165 yards on 40 carries against the Irish.

USC wasn't as formidable as its record indicated — and there was something else. There had been persistent rumors since the previous spring that McKay would accept a multiyear, $2-million package and become coach at Tampa Bay, an NFL expansion team.

McKay conceded that he had talked to Hugh Culverhouse, Tampa Bay's owner, but he had little else to say.

When the rumors resurfaced stronger than ever at midseason, McKay announced, after the Notre Dame game and before his team was to play California at Berkeley, that he would indeed be leaving USC at the end of the 1975 season.

McKay was in the dual role of athletic director and football coach. He had become weary of the politics of college athletics and the recruiting grind after 16 years. And there was precious little more that he could accomplish at the college level. The most compelling reason to leave USC, however, was the lifetime security of the Tampa Bay offer.

McKay's decision had an immediate adverse

After fielding a Jim Jones' aerial, flanker Bob Chandler is slowed by a defender. Chandler led the Trojans in receptions in 1970 with 41 for 590 yards and three touchdowns.

effect on his team, which lost four straight conference games — California, Stanford, Washington and UCLA. It was a shocking reversal of form because USC hadn't lost a conference game since 1971 and hadn't suffered four consecutive defeats since 1958.

Although McKay's announcement probably had a damaging psychological effect on his team, there were other factors in USC's demise. The Trojans had suffered an inordinate number of injuries and they lacked a proven quarterback.

Vince Evans, a former high school tailback, was Haden's replacement. At 6-feet-1-inch and 205 pounds, he was a strong runner, but an erratic passer. At one time during the season, he had completed only 29 percent of his passes, a huge drop from the skilled Haden, who had set school records for most touchdown passes in a career (33) and most completions in a season (137).

To make matters worse, Rob Hertel, Evans' backup and a better pure passer, broke his leg in the fourth game of the season. McKay was forced to start a third-string quarterback, Mike Sanford, against Washington.

Although USC had a disappointing 7-4 regular season record and was out of the Rose

PHOTO BY DICK MARTIN COURTESY OF USC SPORTS INFORMATION

All-American fullback Sam Cunningham extends himself over Illinois linemen to score his first touchdown of the 1971 season. Cunningham usually sacrificed his own great running ability to perform as one of USC's all-time great blocking backs.

Richard Wood means defense . . . in a domineering, omnipresent fashion.

Linebacker Richard Wood (83), USC's only three-time All-American, made 18 individual tackles and one interception in his first varsity appearance against Arkansas. The "Batman," as he was dubbed, was a sophomore on the 1972 Trojans, which is regarded by many as the greatest USC team in history.

Bowl race even before the UCLA game, McKay still went out as a winner.

The Trojans accepted an invitation to play in the Liberty Bowl in Memphis and pulled off a mild upset by defeating Texas A&M, 20-0.

So McKay left. The jaunty man who would walk into his morning press conferences at Heritage Hall, roll a cigar around in his mouth and say, "O.K. gang, we can begin. The star is here," was now gone.

McKay was never comfortable in large groups. But, in the presence of friends and writers he trusted, he could be informative and charming. Sometimes he would spend hours talking football and diagramming plays for a writer at his own special table at Julie's, a restaurant close to the campus that is a hangout for Trojans, past and present.

Others found McKay to be waspish, rude and rabbit-eared. If a publication, no matter how small, knocked him or his teams, he would flare up — but not for long.

He left a legacy of winning, innovative football at USC and he is missed by some Los Angeles writers for his quick wit and droll remarks. McKay was considered good copy. A sampling:

• On football being called a game of emotion: "Nobody is more emotional than my wife and she's a lousy football player."

• At halftime of the 1964 USC-Notre Dame game when the Trojans trailed, 17-0: "Gentlemen, if we don't score more than 17 points in the second half, we don't have a chance."

• Addressing his team before an important game: "In the past, we've asked you men to win for your parents, your girlfriends, your school and the alumni . . . I think it's about time you went out and won one for yourselves."

• Talking about one of his offensive lines: "You've heard of the Seven Blocks of Granite? Last year, we had the Seven Blocks of Cement."

• On people calling him arrogant: "I don't think of myself as arrogant. I think of myself as a friendly horse's ass. What I don't like is when a sportswriter doesn't like me and writes that nobody likes me. That ticks my wife off."

And that was McKay.

Mike Rae sets the offense against Stanford in 1972. The Trojans had lost two in a row to their old rival. This time USC prevailed, 30-21. Rae was honored as MVP on what many consider the greatest Trojan team of all, perhaps the greatest college team ever.

Mike Rae's pitchout starts USC's sweep left against Arkansas. The Trojans were an unknown when they went on the road to open the 1972 season against the Razorbacks, a team with national championship aspirations. When they returned to L.A. with a 31-10 victory, it was the Trojans who were on their way to the title.

Anthony Davis strides toward the goal line as the Buckeyes' Neal Colzie tries to cut him off. Colzie was a "head" late as A.D. high-steps into the end zone for another Trojan tally in the 1973 Rose Bowl.

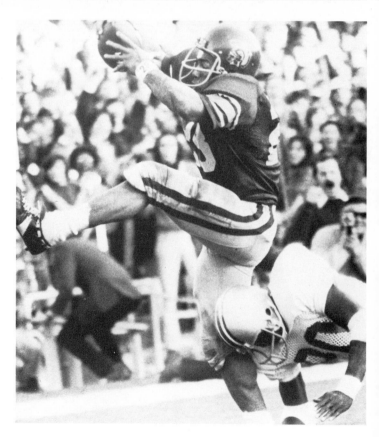

Sam "Bam" Cunningham executes his patented "vault" for one of his four touchdowns against Ohio State in the 1973 Rose Bowl. USC's smashing 42-17 win capped a perfect 12-0 season and the national championship.

Lynn Swann was not only a great receiver but a great runner after catching the ball. That talent made him a dangerous threat as a punt returner as this sequence shows. Swann simply puts a tremendous move on the Georgia Tech defender to avoid what seems to be a sure tackle and go into the end zone standing up.

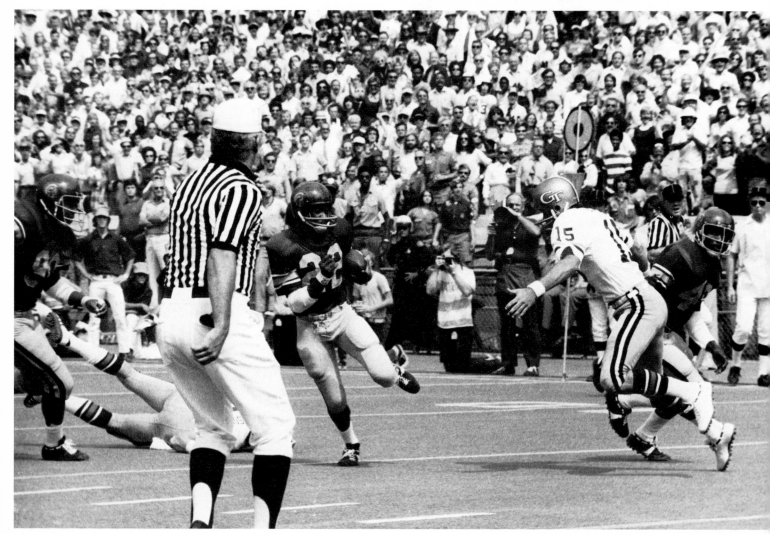

ARNOLD FRAN

94

ARNOLD FRANKEL

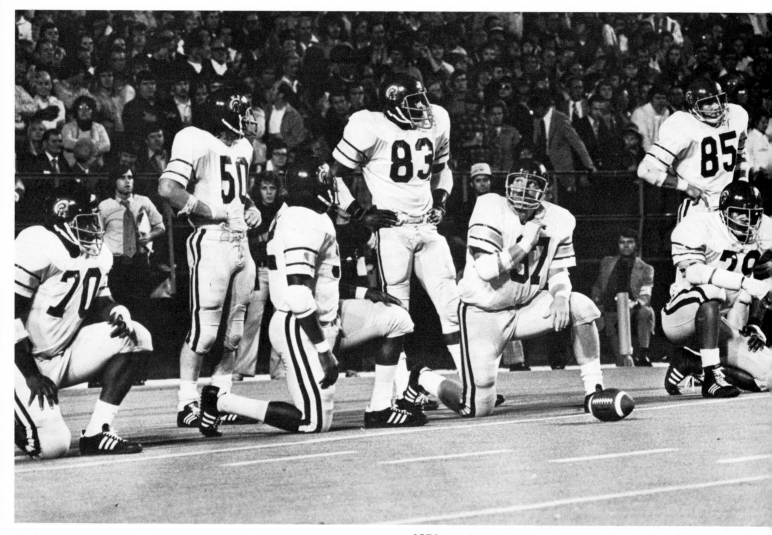

1974 saw the Trojans capture the fourth national championship of John McKay's USC career, much to the credit of this defensive front: Art Riley (70), Kevin Bruce (50), Otha Bradley (92), Richard Wood (83), Tim Rhames (97), Gary Jeter (79) and Dale Mitchell (85).

All-American rover Charles Phillips (49) breaks from the defensive huddle in 1974. The season sees him carry an intercepted fumble for 98 yards and an interception 90.5 yards (an NCAA record) — both against Iowa in a 41-3 Trojan victory.

Rhodes Scholar quarterback Pat Haden prepares to set the 1974 Trojan offense in motion. If anyone ever fit the hero image, it was Haden. And his performance at USC made the image a reality.

Pat Haden's 241 career completions, including 33 that resulted in touchdowns, started out just like this.

How sweet it is when you can celebrate a heart-stopping Rose Bowl victory with an old friend. Pat Haden (left) and Johnny McKay were teammates in high school before moving on together to USC. In fact Haden lived in the McKay home during high school. How fitting that the two could team up on the touchdown pass that put USC in position for its 18-17 win over Ohio State in the 1975 Rose Bowl.

The pass rush as demonstrated by Gary Jeter: Beat your blocker, close on the quarterback, force the fumble. The victim is Purdue quarterback Craig Nagel. Mr. Jeter put on this kind of clinic often enough to gain All-American honors and a Special General Excellence Award given only one time in USC history.

Assistant coach Marv Goux talks things over with coach McKay, as he did often throughout McKay's tenure. Goux, co-captain of the 1955 Trojans, was named an assistant coach in 1957 with numerous defensive standouts benefiting from his tutelage over the years, including 11 first team All-Americans. An inspirational leader, Goux now serves as assistant head coach while continuing to work with the defensive line.

John Who? Trojan fans may have been unsure about the selection of the relatively unknown John Robinson to succeed John McKay in 1976, especially after USC was shocked by Missouri (25-46) in his first game. Four years, four bowl victories, a national championship and two

his own legend to go with those of McKay and Howard Jones. His teams had compiled a 42-6-1 record for an .867 winning percentage, highest in USC history. It is now apparent that Trojan fans had no need for concern in 1976 — the Trojan heritage was being passed into sure

Chapter Six

THE LATEST LEGEND

Howard Jones won his last national championship in 1932. John McKay won his first in 1962. That's a 30-year drought between legendary coaches.

USC wouldn't have to wait that long after McKay resigned.

It's axiomatic in sports that a man who immediately succeeds a living legend is approaching quicksand. Even if he's successful by most standards, his accomplishments will be compared to that of his predecessor. In most instances, they won't measure up.

Al McGuire, the former Marquette basketball coach, says that the coach who replaces a legendary figure is an *interim* coach.

But John Robinson, McKay's replacement, has not only maintained the winning Trojan tradition, he has added a new dimension to the USC football program with his own concepts of the game.

If his first four seasons (1976-1979) indicate what he will accomplish in the future, USC can order now a bust of Robinson to be placed alongside Jones and McKay in Heritage Hall.

Robinson, with a 42-6-1 (.867) record, is the winningest coach, percentagewise, in USC history. Already he has won one national championship in 1978. His teams have finished second in the final wire service polls twice, in 1976 and in 1979.

USC is the No. 1 bowl team in the country, based on most wins (19) and highest winning percentage (.760) — a minimum of 10 bowl appearances. Robinson has made a significant contribution to this statistic. He has won three Rose Bowls (1977, 1979, 1980) and a Bluebonnet Bowl game (New Year's Eve, 1977) for a 4-0 bowl record. Jones was 5-0 in bowl games, McKay 6-3, each of them in 16 seasons at USC. Robinson is ahead of their pace.

As a tactician, he has retained the best from McKay — the "I" formation and tailback-oriented offense along with a sound defense while establishing the quarterback as a more important figure in his offense.

When Robinson became USC's coach in 1976, he said: "For many years the USC tailback has been the best single position in

college football. Now we want to create a similar environment for the quarterback. We're going to make the quarterback position more successful."

McKay's best teams were balanced offensively (running and passing), but, in 1975, when USC slumped, the poor play of quarterback Vince Evans was a contributing factor.

Evans was a much-improved quarterback under Robinson in 1976. Robinson and his offensive staff, particularly quarterback coach Paul Hackett, were responsible for the improvement of Rob Hertel in 1977.

It was in 1978 and 1979 that the quarterback, Paul McDonald, really came into a position of eminence in the USC offense, rivaling that of the tailback, Charles White.

Robinson, like McKay, was a virtually unknown assistant coach when he was named USC's coach. He was a reserve end on Oregon's 1957 Rose Bowl team and he stayed at the school for 12 years as an assistant before becoming McKay's offensive coordinator from 1972 through 1974. He left USC in 1975 to join the Oakland Raiders as an offensive assistant coach.

Robinson, 6-feet-1-inch, 205 pounds, is an enthusiastic and positive-thinking man. He doesn't have the caustic wit of McKay, but he's humorous, interesting and a favorite of the media for his accessibility and candidness.

He is not a grim, "football is life-and-death" coach. He is genuinely interested in his players, both on and off the field, and seems to communicate with them more than McKay did.

McKay coached through his assistants, riding around the practice field in a golf cart to oversee the entire operation.

Robinson relies on his assistants, too, and he has an able staff, including Marv Goux, the defensive line coach and a coaching fixture at USC for 24 years; defensive coordinator Don Lindsey; offensive line coach Hudson Houck; backfield coach John Jackson and Hackett.

Robinson is more involved in the day-to-day practice operation, hustling from one group to the other — praising, scolding and teaching.

Practice makes . . . perfect. In this case the handoff by Rob Hertel.

Robinson reportedly had no hangup about being in the McKay shadow:

"I believe that the key is not getting negative about the other guy," Robinson told Loel Schrader of the Long Beach Press Telegram. "John McKay left a great football tradition at USC and that's very positive. I was smart enough to keep 80 percent of what we had — what McKay had been doing — and smart enough to change about 20 percent."

Born in Chicago and reared in San Mateo, Robinson grew up with John Madden, the former Oakland Raiders head coach. It was Madden who finally prevailed on Robinson to join him at Oakland in 1975.

Madden says Robinson has two qualities that make him a successful coach and a likeable person: "Intelligence and getting along with people. From those two all the other things come out: communication, working with the alumni, recruiting wisely."

Although Robinson has been offered head coaching jobs in pro football, he seems to enjoy thoroughly the college atmosphere at USC. He signed a five-year contract with the school on the eve of USC's 1980 Rose Bowl game with Ohio State and says he intends to stay on the job for at least that long.

"I really missed the Trojan Horse (Traveler III, which gallops around the Coliseum track before every game)," Robinson said on accepting the USC job in 1976. "Yes, really. The horse and band, the song girls. There's a tremendous aura around college football."

But Robinson's first night as a head football coach was a nightmare. That was Sept. 11, 1976, when Missouri, which has a penchant for knocking off top-rated teams, shocked Robinson's Trojans, 46-25, in the opener.

"They (the alumni) probably wanted to get rid of that s.o.b. — me — right then," Robinson recalled.

But the game was hardly a harbinger for the season. The Trojans, who have been upset in the past in openers, got their act together and defeated Oregon, 53-0; Purdue, 31-13; Iowa, 55-0; Washington State, 23-14; Oregon State, 56-0; California, 20-6; Stanford, 48-24, and Washington, 20-3, to set up another Rose Bowl-deciding game with UCLA, unbeaten and ranked No. 2 in the country under new head coach Terry Donahue.

Ricky Bell was the latest model off the USC tailback assembly line that season. He had broken O.J. Simpson's single-season rushing

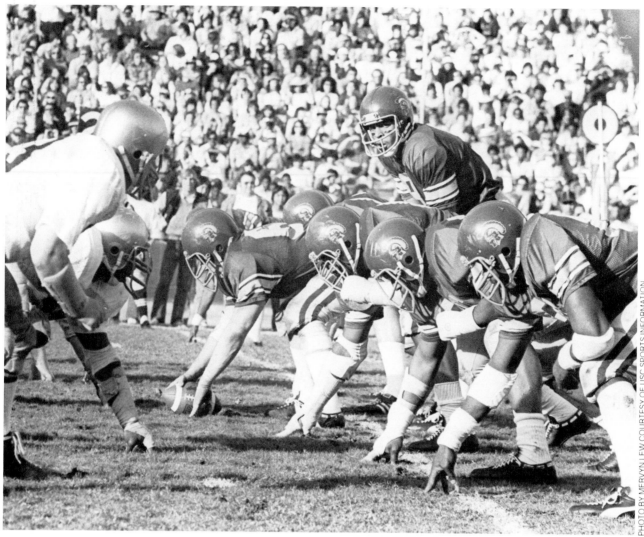

Vince Evans sets his offensive line against Notre Dame. As any Trojan tailback will attest, the USC offensive lines have been precision, often devastating, machines.

record the previous year, gaining 1,957 yards on 385 carries.

Bell didn't fit the mold of a typical USC tailback. Garrett, Clarence Davis, Anthony Davis and, later, White, were relatively short, stocky types. At 6-feet-2-inches and 218 pounds, Bell, a former fullback and linebacker, was a battering, bruising runner with good speed for a big man. He was at his best in a night game against Washington State at Seattle's Kingdome, where he rushed for 347 yards on 51 carries, setting school and conference records. Only Michigan State's Eric Allen had gained more yards (350 in 1971) in a college game.

Bell missed part of the next two games and sat out a third with ankle and hip injuries. Freshman Charles White took his place. It was these injuries that probably kept Bell from seriously challenging Pittsburgh's Tony

Dorsett for the Heisman Trophy — a goal of any worthy USC tailback. Still, he gained 1,433 yards for the season to become USC's No. 2 all-time leading rusher behind Anthony Davis, 3,724 to 3,689.

The productivity of a USC tailback is taken for granted. What was noteworthy was the development of Evans, an unskilled passer in 1975.

Evans completed 54 percent of his passes for 1,440 yards and 10 touchdowns, while Hertel was 65 percent for 452 yards and eight touchdowns. Not only did Evans and Hertel double their passing yardage from 1975, but as a tandem they had 14 more scoring throws.

Already the Robinson influence of a balanced attack was seen. Stanford stacked its defenses to stop USC's strong running game,

Two-time All-American defensive back Dennis Thurman returns an interception against Purdue.

so Evans went to the air and threw four touchdown passes in eliminating the Cardinals from the Rose Bowl race.

Evans had a miserable game against UCLA in 1975, when he misfired on 14 straight passes. But his improvement was apparent in 1976 when he completed seven of 13 for 79 yards and rushed 14 times for 63 yards, including a 36-yard touchdown on a quarterback-draw play. Bell wasn't completely physically sound but he contributed 167 yards on 36 carries.

It was the defense that made the big difference. UCLA's veer offense had averaged 37 points and 361 yards rushing a game, second best in the country. But the Bruins managed only 140 yards against USC and didn't score until the final four minutes. The

Noseguard Harold Steele (71) chases a fumble by Iowa quarterback Butch Caldwell in this action in 1976.

24-14 score was misleading.

USC beat Notre Dame, 17-13, the next week and then the Trojan defense completely destroyed a powerful Michigan in the Rose Bowl. The Wolverines were the nation's leading scoring (39 points average) and rushing team (448 yards), but they could score only six points and rush for 217 yards as USC won, 14-6, without Bell.

Bell was knocked unconscious on USC's first series. White, who would go on to become the school's most prolific rusher, filled in with 114 yards on 32 carries. Evans completed 14 of 20 passes for 181 yards, scored a touchdown on a one-yard keeper and was named Player of the

Ricky Bell hits the hole for some of his 167 yards against UCLA in 1976. The Trojans' 24-14 win over the No. 2 ranked, unbeaten Bruins clinched the Rose Bowl berth in coach John Robinson's first year.

Game.

Robinson became the first rookie head coach from the Pac-8 to win the Rose Bowl game in 61 years. William Dietz had done it for Washington State in 1916 in the second Rose Bowl.

Bell, safety Dennis Thurman, defensive tackle Gary Jeter and offensive tackle Marvin Powell got All-American recognition. USC finished with an 11-1 record and a No. 2 national rating behind undefeated Pittsburgh.

Robinson lost 14 starters from his 1976 team, including Bell, Evans, Jeter, Powell, flanker Shelton Diggs and linebackers David Lewis and Rod Martin. Nonetheless,

Ricky Bell heads upfield against UCLA behind the right side of his line. including tight end William Gay (86).

expectations were high for 1977 because USC had quality replacements.

The Trojans started fast, winning their first four games and moving to the top of the rankings. Alabama snapped USC's 15-game unbeaten streak with a 21-20 victory at the Coliseum and the Trojans suddenly became an inconsistent team. They lost three of their next five games — an embarrassing 49-19 setback to Notre Dame at South Bend, where the Irish switched jerseys before the game to get a psychological advantage, and conference losses to California, 17-14, and Washington, 28-10.

The Trojans were out of the Rose Bowl running by the time they met UCLA. But it was an important game for the Bruins. If they beat USC, they would get the Rose Bowl bid; a loss would send Washington to Pasadena.

In one of the most exciting games of the city series, UCLA took an early 10-0 lead before USC surged ahead, 26-10, in the third quarter. The Bruins countered behind sophomore quarterback Rick Bashore and were leading, 27-26, with only a few minutes remaining.

Hertel, who had been inconsistent at times during the season, began to click on his passes.

Shelton Diggs hauls in one of two USC touchdown passes in the Trojans 17-13 win over Notre Dame in 1976.

Split end Randy Simmrin (18) outdistances Notre Dame's Joe Restic en route to a 63-yard touchdown and, ultimately, coach John Robinson's first victory over the Fighting Irish. Simmrin became USC's all-time leading pass receiver.

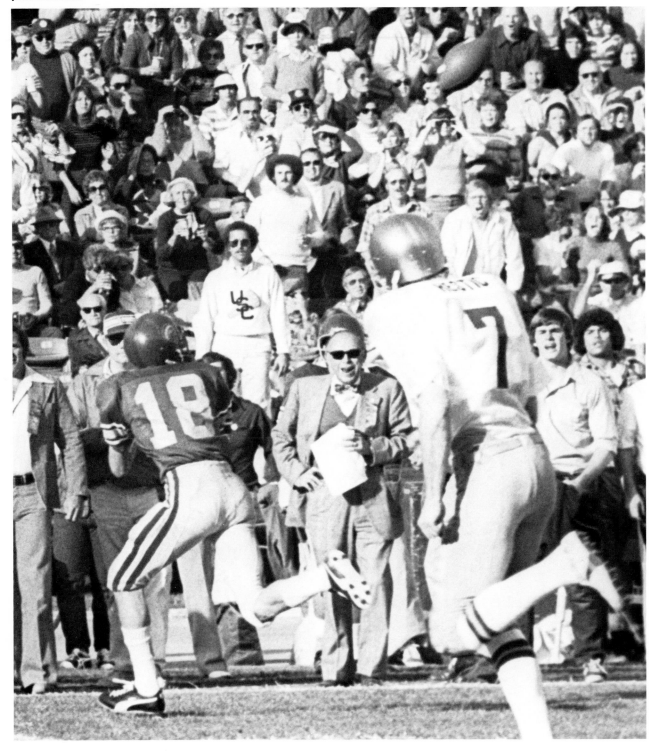

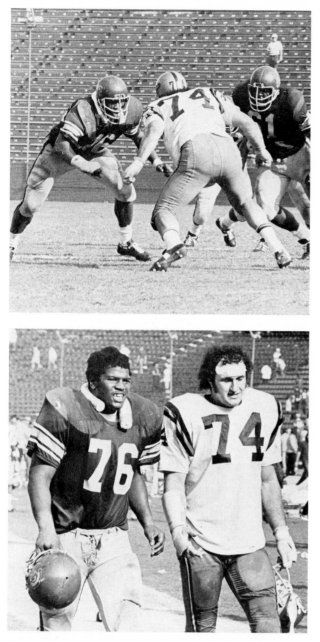

These pictures demonstrate what college football should be all about — fierce competition on the field, mutual respect off the field. The combatants are USC's Marvin Powell (76) and Purdue's Ken Novak (74), both All-Americans.

A long Trojan drive was helped by a pass interference penalty against the Bruins and a key completion to split end Randy Simmrin.

As time was running out, Frank Jordan kicked a 38-yard field goal with two seconds left and he kicked UCLA right out of the Rose Bowl, 29-27.

USC got a consolation prize, a Bluebonnet Bowl bid against Texas A & M at Houston's Astrodome. It was a wild offensive party on New Year's Eve. USC gained 620 yards rushing and passing; A & M gained 519. Hertel's passing (11 of 15, 248 yards and four touchdowns) was decisive and USC won, 47-28.

It was difficult to determine why USC stumbled in 1977 — although many teams would gladly settle for an 8-4 record. Some said Robinson, in his zeal to establish a balanced offense, had Hertel throwing more often than he should and he was intercepted 18 times. The Trojans also lacked some speed on defense.

For a change, USC wasn't highly ranked in the 1978 preseason polls. Nor were the Trojans the consensus favorite to win the newly expanded Pacific 10 with the addition of Arizona and Arizona State. Both UCLA and Washington had impressive credentials.

Robinson had talent, but it was unproven. He returned 10 full-time starters but only 12 seniors among his top 44 players.

"The biggest problem is the uncertainty of our new players and how long it will take them to be comfortable and confident in what they're doing," the USC coach said.

USC's schedule was even more demanding than usual — six bowl teams, including national champion Notre Dame (Cotton), No. 2-rated Alabama (Sugar) and Washington (Rose).

Robinson was counting on the quick development of southpaw quarterback Paul McDonald, who had played in only five previous games in two years while backing up Evans and Hertel.

"Paul is kind of the symbol of our whole team," Robinson said. "We know he'll be good, but when?"

Robinson got his answer in the third game of the season. USC opened with lackluster wins over Texas Tech and Oregon. No. 1-ranked Alabama, reportedly one of Bear Bryant's strongest teams, was waiting for USC in Birmingham.

The Crimson Tide was an 11-point favorite.

Seldom in USC's history had it been relegated to such an underdog status.

But Robinson's young team matured even faster than he could have imagined. The Trojans, with tailback Charles White who was now a junior gaining 199 yards on 29 carries, toppled Alabama, 24-14.

A cool, intelligent McDonald repeatedly changed plays at the line of scrimmage against Alabama's stunting defense. He invariably made the right call. He completed nine of 16 passes for 113 yards including scoring throws of six and 41 yards to Kevin Williams, the small, sprinter flanker.

Fullback Mosi Tatupu shows that he could run as well as block bursting through a big hole against Michigan.

White, who scored USC's first touchdown on a cutback run aided by a block from guard Brad Budde, was praised by Bryant. "I don't remember ever playing against a tailback that can run like White," the Bear said.

USC didn't let down the next week against Michigan State, the Big 10 co-champion. McDonald threw two touchdown passes and White and fullback Lynn Cain gained 82 and 96 yards while playing only three quarters. The Trojans buried the Spartans, 30-9.

The Trojans seemed unbeatable then, but they were walking into a trap at Tempe, Arizona, where the Sun Devils, a former power in the Western Athletic Conference (WAC), were anxious to prove they could play with the established teams of the Pac-10.

Arizona State surprised USC, 20-7, as ASU quarterback Mark Malone accounted for 295 yards in total offense. McDonald mishandled several snaps in the game and the Trojans lost four of seven fumbles. The shoddy ballhandling was due to the loss of four centers because of injuries and a fifth went down in the first quarter, forcing Robinson to put inexperienced players at the position.

USC now was in a bind. UCLA had beaten Washington in the opener, which meant the Trojans couldn't afford to lose another game if they expected to get to the Rose Bowl. They didn't. They beat Stanford, 13-7, and Washington, 28-10, in important conference games. Then they stopped UCLA, 17-10, to get the Rose Bowl bid. The Trojans opened up a 17-0 halftime lead on the Bruins on McDonald's touchdown passes to Calvin

Dwight Ford (22) takes off on the longest run from scrimmage in USC history, 94 yards against Texas A&M in the 1977 Bluebonnet Bowl.

Sweeney and Williams plus a field goal. Then they sat on the lead. UCLA, averaging 273 yards rushing prior to the game, was restricted to only 62 yards.

The Trojans had the Rose Bowl bid but if they were to stay in contention for the national championship, they had to beat their old rival, Notre Dame, the following week at the Coliseum.

The Fighting Irish, coached by Dan Devine, had lost their first two games but had regrouped for an eight-game winning streak.

McDonald threw two touchdown passes and with White on his way to a 205-yard rushing day, USC had Notre Dame reeling and on the ropes, leading them, 24-6, after three quarters.

The Irish, behind quarterback Joe Montana's accurate passing, made a comeback

USC begins its drive to the 1978 national championship as Charles White scores in the 17-9 season-opening win over Texas Tech.

to rival any in the school's illustrious history. Incredibly, Notre Dame scored three touchdowns in the fourth quarter to take a 25-24 lead with 46 seconds remaining.

There was time enough for USC to make an even more amazing comeback. McDonald's 35-yard pass to split end Sweeney and White's short run positioned Jordan for a possible game-winning field goal.

Jordan kicked a 38-yard field goal with two seconds left to beat UCLA in 1977, then booted a 37-yard field goal with *two* seconds remaining to shock Notre Dame, 27-25. It was a bitter defeat for the Irish, who contended that McDonald, while attempting to pass, fumbled and lost the ball on the final drive. An official saw it differently, ruling that the USC quarterback's arm was moving forward, making it an incomplete pass. This play will provoke arguments between Trojan and Irish fans for years to come.

Offensive tackle Anthony Munoz blasts a hapless Texas Tech defender. Munoz could run an amazingly quick 4.9 forty for his 6-feet-7-inches and 280 pounds.

It was on to the Rose Bowl — and more controversy — for USC. By this time, the Pac-8 had taken charge of its series with the Big 2, Michigan and Ohio State, of the Big 10, winning eight of the previous nine Rose Bowl games. The Trojans made it nine of 10 with a 17-10 win over Michigan.

White scored USC's second touchdown in the second quarter on a three-yard dive. At least it was signaled a touchdown. White lost the ball while in flight. Subsequent television replays showed almost conclusively he didn't have the ball when he broke the plane of the goal line.

USC went into the game as the nation's third-ranked team, behind unbeaten Penn State and once-beaten Alabama, in both wire service polls. ABC-TV billed the Sugar Bowl meeting between Penn State and Alabama as the showdown for the national championship. When 'Bama won, it claimed the title, although

The Trojan two-step? USC's Lynn Cain and this California defender seem to be executing a bit of choreography in this action. Cain's 977 yards rushing in 1978 set a record for USC fullbacks.

The Tide had been whipped by USC earlier. As it turned out, both teams were declared national champions. Alabama won comfortably in the AP poll and USC barely won in the UPI balloting.

It was an All-American season for White. Robinson's plan to make the USC quarterback position more successful had been rewarding with McDonald. In his first year as a starter, he tied the school record with 19 touchdown passes, completed 57 percent of his passes for 1,690 yards and had only seven interceptions in 203 attempts. The NCAA had adopted a new quarterback rating system for the 1980 season and, had it been in effect in 1979, McDonald would have been the leading passer in the country.

White, the durable tailback, was already the leading career rusher in Pac-10 history with 4,195 yards and a 5.1 average. He had the

benefit of performing as a freshman and had moved ahead of such famous USC tailbacks as Garrett, Simpson, Anthony Davis and Bell.

If USC was overlooked in preseason ratings in 1978, newspapers, magazines and wire services made up for it in 1979. Everyone was getting on the Trojan bandwagon. But there was more to it than that. People were saying this might be the greatest football team of all time.

Robinson cringed to hear such adulation before USC had played a single game. He pointed out that several key players were healing from surgery, that there was no experienced tailback depth nor a proven fullback and that six of USC's 11 games were on the road.

Still, the Trojans seemed awesome. They were coming off a 12-1 season, a share of the national championship and White and

All-American tailback Charles White (12) conducts aerial reconnaissance over the six-point stripe during USC's 27-25 victory over Notre Dame in 1978. This effort yielded two of White's 205 yards on the day.

Lombardi Award-winning guard Brad Budde (71) leads the way for Heisman Trophy winner Charles White. In 1976, Budde became the first freshman to start a season opener since World War II.

McDonald, now seniors, represented the best one-two offensive punch in college football.

USC had been a young team in 1978 but now Robinson had 15 returning starters — eight on offense, seven on defense. Besides White and McDonald, Robinson had such skilled players as offensive tackle Anthony Munoz (6-feet-7-inches, 280 pounds) and guard Brad Budde (6-feet-5-inches, 253 pounds), both All-American prospects; wide receiver Kevin (Bug) Williams, who in two seasons had 13 touchdowns on 27 catches, a 20.5-yard average; three experienced tight ends — Hoby Brenner, James Hunter and Vic Rakhshani; such proven down linemen as Myron Lapka, Ty Sperling and Dennis Edwards; mobile linebackers in Dennis Johnson who was another All-American prospect and Larry

McGrew and two of the nation's best safeties, Ron Lott and Dennis Smith.

USC struggled some to beat Texas Tech, 21-7, at Lubbock, a game in which Munoz was knocked out for the season with torn knee ligaments and White bruised his shoulder.

The Trojans then beat Oregon State and Minnesota with ridiculous ease, compiling halftime scores of 35-3 and 35-0, which allowed third- and fourth-stringers to play extensively.

It was during the 48-14 win over Minnesota that Duffy Daugherty, the former Michigan State coach, rushed breathlessly into a radio booth and declared that USC was the most impressive football team he had *ever* seen.

Then, LSU's Charley McClendon, whose team would meet the Trojans the next week in

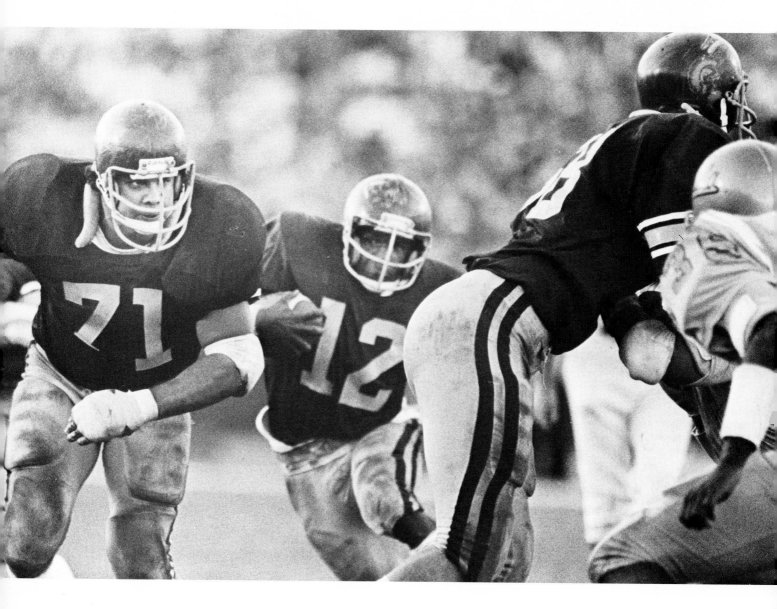

Myron Lapka (96) was a rare three-year starter at defensive tackle for the Trojans. He racked up 125 tackles in his last two seasons as USC boasted one of the country's top defensive units.

Brad Budde (71) and Keith Van Horne execute a cross-blocking maneuver to spring Charles White against UCLA.

Baton Rouge, poured some more syrup: "USC is the best team in the country — right after the Steelers and Cowboys."

But Robinson knew that such talk was seductive and that playing any LSU team at Tiger Stadium, known as Death Valley, was an ordeal for a visiting team.

South Bend is considered a pit because of the crowd noise and ardent Irish fans, but Roger Valdiserri, Notre Dame's sports information director, who had accompanied Notre Dame teams to Baton Rouge, told the Trojans: "Our place is a kindergarten compared to LSU."

Valdiserri wasn't exaggerating. A raucous crowd taunted USC with its "Tiger Bait" chant. The LSU band played so loudly when the Trojans had the ball that McDonald's

All-American linebacker Dennis Johnson brings Stanford's Jim Brown to a crushing halt.

signals couldn't be heard.

And an inspired LSU team, which always plays better at home, led USC, 12-3, after three quarters. The Trojans showed their class by scoring 14 points in the final quarter. The winning touchdown came on an eight-yard pass from McDonald to Williams with 32 seconds left. The Trojans escaped Death Valley with a 17-12 win and their No.1 rating still intact.

Two weeks later USC lost its No. 1 ranking in an improbable manner. Stanford, traditionally known as a sophisticated passing team without much of a running game or a robust defense, was the spoiler.

There was no indication, however, in the first half of this USC Homecoming game at the Coliseum that Stanford would offer much

Paul McDonald cocks to throw against California in USC's 24-14 win in 1979. He was even rougher on Cal the previous year, stinging the Golden Bears for four TD passes tying a school record.

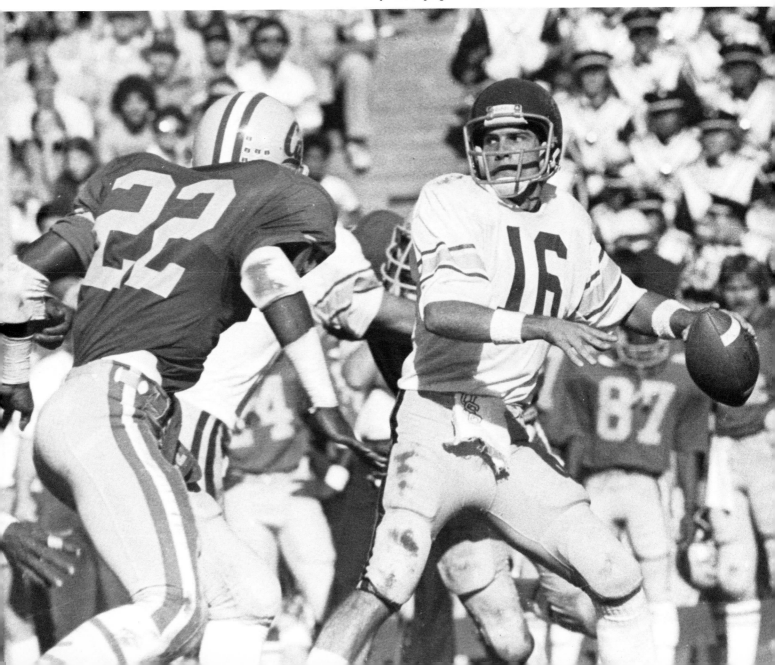

opposition. The Trojans easily, perhaps too easily, moved out to a 21-0 lead at halftime. A rout seemed imminent.

The Cardinals, behind the passing of quarterback Turk Schonert, stunned USC with 21 points in the second half and the game ended in a tie.

USC was no longer awesome and Stanford had exposed a flaw in the Trojan defense. A good passing team could move on USC.

Notre Dame proved as much the following week by gaining 535 yards on USC, 286 by passing.

USC's offense was even more productive with 591 total yards — the most ever gained against a Notre Dame team.

It was offensive football at its best, another thrilling Trojan-Irish encounter on national television. But USC had the ultimate offensive weapons in White and McDonald and they couldn't be contained. White gained 261 yards

The greatest one-two punch in USC history. Charles White and Paul McDonald own almost every Trojan rushing and passing record, quite a testament to John Robinson's philosophy of equal emphasis on the quarterback and tailback.

on 44 carries, passed the 1,000 mark for the season and moved into third place on the NCAA's all-time rushing list. McDonald passed 311 yards for a career high while completing 21 of 32 for two touchdowns and no interceptions. The Trojans won it, 42-23.

Great football teams in the past have had an outstanding running attack or a superlative passing offense, but not the capacity to do both exceptionally well.

Robinson had developed a one-two punch that was virtually indefensible. Frank Broyles, the former Arkansas coach, who was a television commentator for the USC-Notre Dame game, said that USC's style of attack is the toughest of all to defend against.

"The Trojans are awesome — with a most uncommon offense based on a combination of runs and passes," Broyles added. "I don't know any coach who has done more than John Robinson with the combination. That's what

Paul McDonald takes the snap from Chris Foote in USC's 34-7 win over Arizona in 1979. McDonald had a field day, setting Trojan single-game records for most completions (25), most yards passing (380) and most yards running and passing (362).

makes the Trojans so hard to beat and so exciting to watch."

USC had had its letdown for the season — that second half against Stanford — and it didn't falter again as it defeated California, 24-14; Arizona, 34-7; Washington, 24-17, and UCLA, 49-14.

After a hard-earned win over the Huskies at Seattle, the Trojans were under the impression that they had clinched the Rose Bowl bid. However, a subsequent Pac-10 ruling forced Arizona State to forfeit all of its wins for the season (including one over Washington) for using ineligible players. So Washington was back in the Rose Bowl race with a 5-1 record instead of 4-2.

"It seems that the team most severely penalized is USC," said Robinson.

USC was required to clinch the Rose Bowl bid a second time by beating UCLA. The Huskies, who benefited from a Trojan victory over the Bruins in 1977 and would have gone to the Rose Bowl in 1979 if UCLA had beaten USC, had their hopes dashed early.

USC put UCLA away quickly with 35 points in the first half. White scored a Pac-10 record-tying four touchdowns.

In 1912, Owen Bird named USC's team the Trojans because they played under "terrific handicaps." He called attention to their fighting spirit, their ability to overcome all obstacles and to carry the fight to the end. Michael Hayes suffered injuries, a change of position, and playing in the shadow of Charles White. Yet he never quit, and when he finally got his chance, the reserve tailback responded with this 54-yard touchdown run against UCLA, aided by blocking from wide receiver Raymond Butler. The spirit of the Michael Hayeses through the years, as much as the Drurys, Garretts, Simpsons and Whites, is what has built The Trojan Heritage.

The Trojans were back in the Rose Bowl for an unprecedented 23rd time and 10th time in the past 14 years.

Ohio State was a familiar opponent, but the Buckeyes were now coached by Earle Bruce, who had replaced the controversial and cantankerous Woody Hayes.

Pac-10 teams, particularly USC, had dominated Ohio State and Michigan in the Rose Bowl the past decade. The Big 10 teams were running-oriented and, if they fell behind, they didn't have a sufficiently skilled passing attack to catch up.

But Purdue and Michigan State, taking the Big 10 lead, had become more pass-conscious and Bruce had one of the nation's most gifted quarterbacks in sophomore Art Schlichter.

The Trojans had been vulnerable against a good passer all season and the poised Schlichter knocked USC off balance as he completed 11 of 21 passes for 297 yards and one touchdown.

With 5:21 to play, the Buckeyes led, 16-10, and the Trojans were in deep trouble at their own 17-yard line.

White, who was already the runaway winner in the Heisman Trophy balloting, simply ran through Ohio State.

In what Rose Bowl historians remember as the Charles White drive, the Trojan tailback gained 71 yards of an 83-yard stay-on-the-ground assault climaxed by his diving touchdown inches away from the goal line.

The successful conversion enabled USC to preserve its unbeaten record, 11-0-1, and it marred a previously unbeaten season for Ohio State (11-1), which had come into the game ranked No. 1 in the Associated Press poll.

The Trojans had pre-Rose Bowl rankings of No. 2 (UPI) and No. 3 (AP) and wound up as the nation's No. 2 team in both polls as Alabama clinched the national championship with a 24-9 victory over Arkansas in the Sugar Bowl.

White and McDonald had superb seasons. White was the nation's leading rusher in 1979. He wound up his regular season career with 5,598 yards — second highest total in NCAA history. McDonald set 17 NCAA, Pac-10 and school passing records. All-American guard Brad Budde won the Lombardi Award as the nation's best lineman and linebacker Dennis Johnson also won All-American honors.

White's successor already was being groomed in 1979. Sophomore Marcus Allen got his apprenticeship playing fullback. He gained 649 yards (5.7 average) and scored eight touchdowns along with 22 pass receptions for 314 yards.

These credentials suggested that Allen would become a tailback worthy of his legacy — from Kaer to Drury to Saunders to Shaver to Mohler to Warburton to Gifford to Arnett to Garrett to Simpson to Anthony Davis to Bell to White.

The University of Southern California celebrated its centennial year in 1980. If the following 100 years of Trojan football are comparable to the first century, it will be, indeed, an inspiring and exciting era.

What better way to begin celebrating USC's centennial year than with a final-moment comeback victory in the 1980 Rose Bowl.

127

Johnny Baker, an All-American tackle, kicked his way into immortality with a 33-yard field goal with one minute to play to beat Notre Dame, 16-14, in 1931. The comeback win is still considered by many Trojan followers as the greatest in USC history.

Chapter Seven
THE 50-YEAR WAR

One week of each year for many years, a special glint has come into the dark eyes of Marv Goux, USC's long-time assistant coach. His jaw becomes more set, his walk is brisker and his voice, on the practice field, has a more emotional edge.

Goux. Former USC linebacker. Spirit enforcer of the Trojans. A man McKay, then Robinson, needed and still need when the team is to be fired up for a particular game.

But there's only ONE game that means more to USC, year-in and year-out, than any other. That's the annual meeting with Notre Dame.

"Gentlemen," Goux will tell the team, "this will be the most memorable experience of your life. It's big man against big man . . . best in the West against the best in the East. A chill will run up and down your spine when you run out of the tunnel, whether it's the Coliseum or Notre Dame Stadium. There's nothing like it."

He wasn't exaggerating.

It is the best long-running show in collegiate football. A fixture on national television. The most prestigious intersectional series in the country. A 50-year war.

The series began in 1926 and the beginning matched two coaching giants of the day, Notre Dame's Knute Rockne and USC's Howard Jones. Except for World War II years, the teams have met every season — in the autumn at South Bend when the leaves are turning golden brown or in the sunshine of the Coliseum in late November or early December.

The winner of the USC-Notre Dame game has won the national championship outright or gone on to become No. 1 no less than 22 times.

It is a rivalry in which exciting games are routine, the unexpected always possible and the caliber of the performances superb.

USC and Notre Dame delight in spoiling previously undefeated seasons for each other or in rearranging the national rankings.

The Trojans stunned the unbeaten Irish in 1931 (16-14), 1938 (13-0), 1948 (14-14 tie), 1964 (20-17) and 1970 (38-28).

Notre Dame marred USC's record in 1927 (7-6), 1947 (38-7), 1952 (9-0), 1968 (21-21 tie) and 1973 (23-14).

The 1928 edition of the Trojans holds two important distinctions. They were the first USC team to beat Notre Dame, and the first to win the national championship.

In 1927 the largest crowd ever to watch a college football game, an estimated 120,000, was in Chicago's Soldier Field for the USC-Notre Dame game. Two years later in Soldier Field, the game attracted 112,912. The 104,953 fans who saw the Trojans play the Irish in 1947 remains the largest crowd in Coliseum history.

Hundreds of All-Americans, including Heisman Trophy winners, have played in this game. There were others, unknown at the time, who achieved a measure of fame for their contributions.

Some of the names that stir memories from both sides:

Notre Dame — Art Parisien, Bucky O'Connor, Marchy Schwartz, Frank Carideo, Moose Krause, Joe Kurth, Bill Shakespeare, Wayne Milner, Andy Pilney, Joe Benoir, Milt Piepul, Angelo Bertelli, Bob Dove, Creighton Miller, Coy McGee, Johnny Lujack, Bill Fischer, Emil Sitko, Leon Hart, George Connor, Ziggy Czraboski, Jim Martin, Bill Gay, Johnny Lattner, Ralph Guglielmi, Paul Hornung, Nick Buoniconti, John Huarte, Jack Snow, Jim Lynch, Kevin Hardy, George Kunz, Joe Theismann, Dave Casper, Mike Fanning, Luther Bradley, Eric Penick, Ken MacAfee, Tom Burgmeier, Vagas Ferguson and Joe Montana.

USC — Mort Kaer, Don Williams, Jeff Cravath, Morley Drury, Jess Hibbs, Francis Tappaan, Russ Saunders, Orv Mohler, Gus Shaver, Johnny Baker, Erny Pinckert, Ray Sparling, Ernie Smith, Cotton Warburton, Aaron Rosenburg, Bud Langley, Grenny Lansdell, Harry Smith, Ollie Day, Bobby Robertson, Ralph Heywood, John Ferraro, Jack Kirby, Bill Martin, Volney Peters, Frank Gifford, Pat Cannamela, Jim Sears, Jon Arnett, Marlin and Mike McKeever, Craig Fertig, Rod Sherman, O.J. Simpson, Adrian Young, Anthony Davis, Pat Haden, Johnny McKay, Gary Jeter, Marvin Powell, Ricky Bell, Brad Budde, Paul McDonald and Charles White.

If it had not been for the persuasiveness of a young bride in 1925, the USC-Notre Dame series may never have been inaugurated.

Gwynn Wilson was USC's graduate manager at the time. He remembers the circumstances better than anyone else. He should.

"I knew that Notre Dame was going to break with Nebraska and there would be an opening on their schedule," Wilson recalled. "Notre Dame was going to play Nebraska at Lincoln on Thanksgiving Day and I thought if I went back there and talked to Rock (Knute Rockne), there might be a chance for us to get a game."

But Wilson first had to convince Harold Stonier, USC's executive secretary and one of Chancellor Rufus B. von KleinSmid's top administrators. He didn't have to do much convincing because Stonier believed it was about time that USC, then a growing school, should try to become nationally

As important as Johnny Baker's winning field goal in the great 1931 win over Notre Dame was the running of Gus Shaver. Shifting from quarterback to fullback, he scored both USC touchdowns to close the Trojans' deficit to 13-14.

prominent in football. Up to that time, USC had scheduled very few intersectional games — the most notable being the 14-3 win over Penn State in the 1923 Rose Bowl game — and had not traveled East.

Stonier agreed to Wilson's plan to meet Rockne, but the 26-year-old graduate manager had still another request.

"I asked Harold if it would be all right if I took my wife along because we had been married only six months," Wilson said. "Those things weren't being done in those days. We didn't have big expense accounts, but he said yes."

So Wilson and his bride, Marion, got on the Sunset Limited to Lincoln. Mission: a USC-Notre Dame home-and-home series.

There were additional factors that favored such a meeting, such as the friendly rivalry between Howard Jones and Rockne when the USC coach was at Iowa.

"I went to the hotel where Rock was staying, but he told me he didn't have enough time to talk about my proposal but said he'd get a ticket for me and my wife on his train going to

The USC-Notre Dame series has seen great performances by great stars on both sides. Fortunately for Trojan fans, some of Notre Dame's great performances have come in losing causes. One example is this great 59-yard run by Paul Hornung in 1955 as he gets by Doug Kranz. Irish fumbles and great efforts by Jon Arnett and C.R. Roberts turned the tide in USC's favor in this game.

Chicago and we could talk then.''

It probably didn't help Wilson's cause that Notre Dame had been shut out by Nebraska, 17-0, but the Wilsons were wedged into a lower berth in the team car and still hopeful.

''I didn't really get a chance to talk to Rock until the afternoon when we went out into the observation car,'' Wilson said. ''He told me that he couldn't meet USC because Notre Dame was traveling too much and the team had gotten the nickname the 'Ramblers' which he didn't like. He also said he was now getting some games with the Western Conference (Big 10).

''I thought the whole thing was off but as Rock and I talked, Marion was with Mrs. Rockne, Bonnie, in her compartment. Marion told Bonnie how nice Southern California was and how hospitable the people were.

''Well, when Rock went back to the compartment, Bonnie talked him into the game. He came back out, looked me up and said, 'What kind of proposition do you have?' I said we'll give you a $20,000 guarantee. He said he would talk to Father Matthew Walsh (Notre Dame's president) and get back to me. He did and the series was on with the first game to be played in the Coliseum on December 4, 1926.

''But if it hadn't been for Mrs. Wilson talking to Mrs. Rockne, there wouldn't have been a series.''

To pick out the most thrilling, most significant or unusual games in the series is to invite argument. Someone will always say, ''Well, you forgot about the time in so and so year, that so and so did that!''

But there have been some memorable meetings:

1926 — Rockne had one of his strongest teams. The Irish won their first seven games, allowing only one touchdown. But Rockne

wasn't with his team when it met Carnegie Tech in Pittsburgh. The famed coach was in Chicago scouting the Army-Navy game. He was due for a shock because Carnegie Tech, aroused by the Notre Dame coach's slight, upset the Irish, 19-0. The Irish weren't overlooking the Trojans. USC had an 8-1 record, losing only to Stanford, 13-12.

A sellout crowd of 76,000 (the Coliseum was later enlarged for the 1932 Olympic Games) was present for the game. Notre Dame scored first: in the second quarter quarterback Charles Riley ran 16 yards around the end. Harry O'Boyle kicked the extra point, although his try was partially blocked by USC center Jeff Cravath.

The Trojans countered when All-American quarterback Mort Kaer scored from the one after setting up the touchdown with a 38-yard pass to end Al Behrendt. Guard Brice Taylor, USC's first All-American, had his extra point try blocked.

In the fourth quarter, USC drove 57 yards to a touchdown with substitute quarterback Don Williams carrying the ball nine straight times. Again, the extra point try failed as Morley Drury's attempt hit an upright.

There were only six minutes left and Notre Dame was on its own 42-yard line when Rockne replaced Riley with Art Parisien, a 148-pound quarterback, who wasn't expected to play. Parisien was injured earlier in the season and Rockne reportedly had allowed the little quarterback to make the trip West as a kindly gesture.

Parisien, a sharp-passing left-hander, threw a 35-yard pass to Butch Niemiec. A few plays later, Parisien from the USC 23 found Niemiec open again for a touchdown. Cravath blocked the extra point try, but the damage had been done: Notre Dame, 13, USC, 12.

1931 — "NOTRE DAME STADIUM (South Bend, Ind.), Nov. 21 (Exclusive) — When Howard Jones is old and a darn sight grayer than now he will tell his grandchildren about the heroic fight his 1931 Trojans made against the undefeated Irish of Notre Dame. He will tell them . . ."

The above is an excerpt from Los Angeles Times columnist Braven Dyer's lead about a game that is still regarded by many USC alumni as the greatest victory in the school's history. Not only that, the game is regarded by college football historians as one of the most dramatic *ever* played.

In the spring of 1931 Rockne had died in a plane crash in Kansas. The team he left to Hunk Anderson was considered a typical Notre Dame powerhouse of the time, a sure-fire national champion.

The Fighting Irish were riding a 26-game unbeaten streak and were substantially favored to beat USC, which had won six straight after an opening 13-7 loss to St. Mary's.

The odds seem justified. Notre Dame, with Marchy Schwartz and Steve Banas making sizeable gains, moved to a 14-0 lead after three quarters. Such an advantage was considered insurmountable in those days because rules inhibited the passing game.

After Notre Dame's second touchdown in the third quarter, an incident occurred that turned the game around from an emotional and tactical standpoint.

USC fullback Jim Musick suffered a broken nose on a short yardage run and was helped off

After a splendid play on Saturday, the 1931 Trojans look resplendent on Sunday as they pose in derby hats on Michigan Avenue (Chicago) celebrating their classic victory over Notre Dame the day before.

the field. His Trojan teammates were incensed and believed that the Irish were guilty of foul play.

Orv Mohler replaced Musick, but not at fullback. Mohler became the quarterback with Gus Shaver shifting from quarterback to fullback. This combination was to prove devastating.

With Mohler and Shaver alternately making consistent yardage, the Trojans moved to a first down on the Irish 14 as the third quarter ended.

Then, early in the final quarter, Ray Sparling fooled the Irish defense on a reverse that carried to the one-yard line. Shaver got the touchdown on his second try, but Johnny Baker's extra point attempt was blocked.

On USC's next series, a pass interference penalty against Notre Dame and the running of Mohler and Shaver enabled the Trojans to reach the Irish 10-yard line. The Sparling reverse was one of Howard Jones' pet plays. Now he had another one up his sleeve. Mohler drove hard into the line and then tossed a lateral to Shaver, who ran away from the flow of the play, scoring on a dive into the corner of the end zone. Baker made the extra point this time but, with eight minutes left, USC seemed fated to lose once again by one point to Notre Dame.

Two minutes remained. USC, still trailing, 14-13, had possession on its own 27. Shaver fired a long pass to Sparling who made a miraculous, fingertip grab at the Irish 40. A few plays later, Jones fooled the Irish on another favorite play. Bob Hall caught a pass from Shaver that carried to the 18-yard line on a tackle-eligible maneuver.

The Trojans worked the ball to the 12. Sparling lost three yards. A pass fell incomplete. At this juncture, Jones sent Homer Griffith into the game believing that Mohler wasn't going to call for a field goal. But captain Stan Williamson waved Griffith back to the bench.

Mohler knew what he was doing. He held the ball as Baker, a tackle, kicked it between the uprights from the 23-yard line. USC had made an amazing comeback for a 16-14 lead with one minute remaining. That's how it ended.

The Trojans celebrated in their locker room and celebrated the next day when the traveling party bought derby hats at a Chicago establishment on Michigan Boulevard.

And when the USC football team returned

to Los Angeles it was greeted by a crowd of 300,000, which cheered the conquering heroes in a ticker tape parade in the downtown area.

No one in sophisticated Los Angeles has seen anything like it since.

1948 — Any discussion of great college football teams would prominently mention Notre Dame's post-World War II teams coached by Frank Leahy. Leahy had restored the Irish to the premier position of prominence they enjoyed under Rockne.

His 1946 team was undefeated, but tied by a strong Army team led by Doc Blanchard and Glenn Davis. His 1947 was unbeaten and untied. When Leahy brought his Fighting Irish into the Coliseum to play USC in 1948, he had another undefeated team, 9-0, and a 26-0-1 record since 1946.

Moreover, since Jones died in 1940, USC was no longer competitive with Notre Dame. The Trojans hadn't beaten the Irish since 1939 and Notre Dame had a commanding 12-6-1 lead in the series.

USC, coached by Jeff Cravath, brought a 6-3

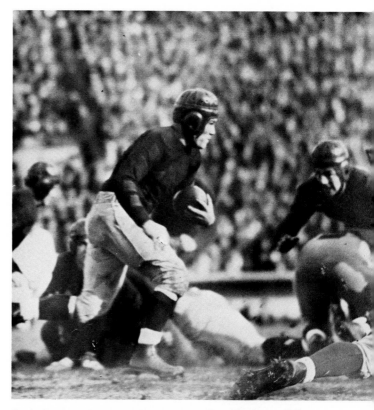

Davie Davis picks up yardage against Notre Dame in 1935. Davis led USC in rushing the following season.

record into the Notre Dame game. It was a good USC team, but hardly outstanding. The Trojans were considered a three-touchdown underdog.

USC, playing one of its most inspiring games in the Cravath era, outplayed Notre Dame most of the game.

The Irish scored first when 250-pound end Leon Hart took a short pass and literally ran over four Trojan defenders while bulling 40 yards to the end zone.

Notre Dame's 7-0 halftime lead didn't hold up. USC, led by quarterback Dean Hill and running backs "Battleship" Bill Martin, Jack Kirby and Art Battle and helped by an aroused defense, scored twice in the second half. Martin got the scores on short line smashes and became only the third Trojan to score two touchdowns on Notre Dame in one game.

An astounding upset was imminent when USC prepared to kick off to Notre Dame late in the game. But Notre Dame, unbeaten through 27 games, remained confident.

In the definitive book on the series, *Notre Dame vs. USC*, written by Cameron Applegate, it is reported that Notre Dame halfback Billy Gay approached the referee and said, "How much time is left?" The referee replied, "Two minutes and 35 seconds." Gay answered, "Thank you sir, that's enough."

Indeed it was enough. Gay returned the kickoff 86 yards to the USC 13-yard line. On third down quarterback Bob Williams' pass, intended for Gay, was incomplete in the end zone, but USC was cited for pass interference. Inexplicably, the ball was placed on the two-yard line instead of the one, where Emil Sitko got the touchdown on second down. Steve Oracko made the extra point and the Irish had escaped with a tie and their long winning streak was still intact.

But USC had the satisfaction of knowing that it had deprived Leahy of a third straight national championship as Michigan wound up as the nation's No. 1 team.

1964 — Dynamic Ara Parseghian, in his first season as Notre Dame coach, had taken a team that went 2-7-1 the previous year and turned it

The USC-Notre Dame series has produced some of the biggest crowds in college football history. The 1948 game drew over 100,000 fans to the Coliseum to see USC, a three-touchdown underdog, battle one of Notre Dame's greatest teams to a 14-14 tie.

into a smooth, unbeaten machine.

The Irish had won nine straight games, outscored the opposition, 270 to 57, holding seven teams to a touchdown or less. They had a balanced, fast-striking offense led by John Huarte, the Heisman Trophy winning quarterback, and his favorite receiver, Jack Snow. Huarte had thrown 15 touchdown passes, while Snow had caught 50 of the quarterback's passes.

It was understandable that Notre Dame, on the verge of its first national championship since 1949, would be a 12-point favorite over USC.

Although USC's record was only 6-3, John McKay had some skilled offensive players, including tailback Mike Garrett, quarterback Craig Fertig, and wide receivers Rod Sherman and Fred Hill.

The USC coach reasoned he could move on Notre Dame if he could keep the hard-rushing Irish from harassing Fertig. Notre Dame shot eight players at a quarterback — four linemen and four linebackers — so McKay decided to keep nine players in to block, sending out a single receiver, Sherman or Hill. McKay laid out three alternate routes for the receivers. Fertig would wait for them to break free. McKay called his play "The Notre Dame Pass."

The Trojans moved the ball on the Irish in the first half but mistakes kept them from scoring. Fertig overthrew an open receiver in the end zone and Hill dropped another pass that was an apparent touchdown.

Notre Dame put 17 points on the board — a field goal, Bill Wolski's five-yard run and Huarte's 21-yard pass to Snow. The Irish seemed assured of their national championship at halftime, leading 17-0. And Parseghian scrawled a message on a blackboard in the locker room: "Only 30 more minutes."

USC, not Notre Dame, took advantage of those 30 minutes. The Trojans, confident of their ability to move the ball, drove 66 yards to a touchdown at the outset of the second half. Garrett cracked over from the one-yard line.

The Irish began to stop themselves. They lost the ball on the USC nine on a wild Huarte pitchout. An Irish touchdown was nullified by a holding penalty.

Fertig passed the Trojans to another touchdown in the fourth quarter. The score came on a 23-yard shot to Hill. USC missed the conversion. Notre Dame still led, 17-13.

ARNOLD FRANKEL

John McKay and Ara Parseghian both took over programs that had slipped a bit from their glory days. But under their guidance, USC and Notre Dame returned to the top of college football. And often as not, national championships once again hinged on the outcome of their annual war.

With 2:10 left in the game, USC had the ball at the Notre Dame 40, the result of a short Irish punt. Fertig hit Hill for a 23-yard gain to the Irish 17. A two-yard Garrett run and two incompletions left the Trojans with a fourth down and eight yards to go.

Sherman insisted he could get open and beat the man covering him. McKay sent the wide receiver into the game with that purpose in mind.

Sherman delayed at the line, faked outside turning cornerback Tony Carey the wrong way and then cut down the middle. Fertig's perfect pass was waiting at the three-yard line and Sherman gathered it in and spun away to score.

The Trojans had taken away another national championship from the Irish just as they had done in 1931, 1938 and 1948.

In the McKay book, *A Coach's Story,* the USC coach recalled that Father Theodore

During the waning minutes of the 1964 Notre Dame war, Rob Sherman fields this strike (one of 90 catches during his Trojan career) from quarterback Craig Fertig. After making the grab on the three-yard line. Sherman spun into the end zone for the touchdown and a USC victory (20-17). The loss cost Ara Parseghian's Irish the national championship.

The "Juice" on the loose. O.J. breaks away for some of his 169 yards against Notre Dame in 1967. His three touchdowns in USC's 24-7 win stamped him as a sure All-American in his first season. Escorting O.J. is flanker Jim Lawrence (28). Notice Simpson's eyes as he seems to set up his blockers and the defenders ahead.

137

Hesburgh, the Notre Dame president, congratulated him, saying, "That wasn't a very nice thing for a Catholic (McKay) to do." McKay replied, "Father, it serves you right for hiring a Presbyterian (Parseghian)."

1974 — Quarterback Pat Haden said it was pure fantasy. Tailback Anthony Davis called it the greatest, the most incredible of all games, adding, "We turned into madmen."

The USC players weren't exaggerating in trying to describe a game that was — and is — one of a kind. Shocking. Amazing. Mystifying. Improbable. All of the adjectives fit.

USC and Notre Dame were formidable teams in 1974 with similar regular-season records. The Trojans were 8-1-1. They had been upset by Arkansas in the opener. The Irish were 9-1, losing only to their nemesis, Purdue.

The Trojans had already accepted a bid to play in the Rose Bowl. The Irish were headed for the Orange Bowl. Both teams still had a chance to move up to No. 1 in the final wire service rankings so the stakes were high.

USC was a four-point favorite, but Notre Dame was the more motivated team in the first half.

Quarterback Tom Clements completed nine of 12 passes for 134 yards and the Irish moved easily in front, 24-0. USC scored on a seven-

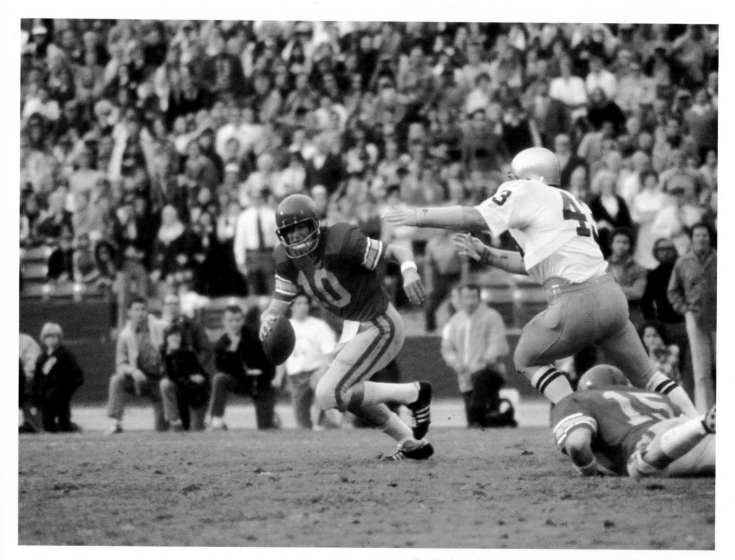

Pat Haden sidesteps the hard-rushing Fighting Irish. Haden escaped to hurl four touchdown passes to help rally USC from 0-24 to win, 55-24, in 1974, perhaps the wildest game in this storied series.

All-American tailback Anthony Davis (28) left dozens of Fighting Irish in his wake, as well as memorable individual statistics, in USC's 1972 and 1974 victories. Davis scored 11 touchdowns against Notre Dame alone, with three of them (96, 97 and 102 yards) following Fighting Irish kickoffs.

yard Haden pass to Davis just before the half ended. The Trojans, trailing 24-6, seemed hopelessly beaten. They were down 18 points and had to play catch-up against the nation's No. 1 defensive team, which had yielded a total of eight touchdowns in its nine previous games.

Notre Dame kicked off to USC at the start of the second half. Davis fielded the ball two yards deep in the end zone, angled toward the sideline, got clearing blocks from Mosi Tatupu and Mario Celotto and won the race to the end zone.

It was the same Davis who had scored *six*

touchdowns against Notre Dame in the 1972 game, including kickoff scoring runs of 97 yards and 96 yards. He had burned the Irish again. More important, his run had a catalytic effect on his teammates and on a Coliseum crowd of 83,552 that started screaming and never stopped.

The events that followed translate into the most astonishing single quarter of football ever played, considering the caliber of the teams.

Davis scored two more times, both on short runs. Haden threw touchdown passes of 18 yards and 45 yards to Johnny McKay, his high

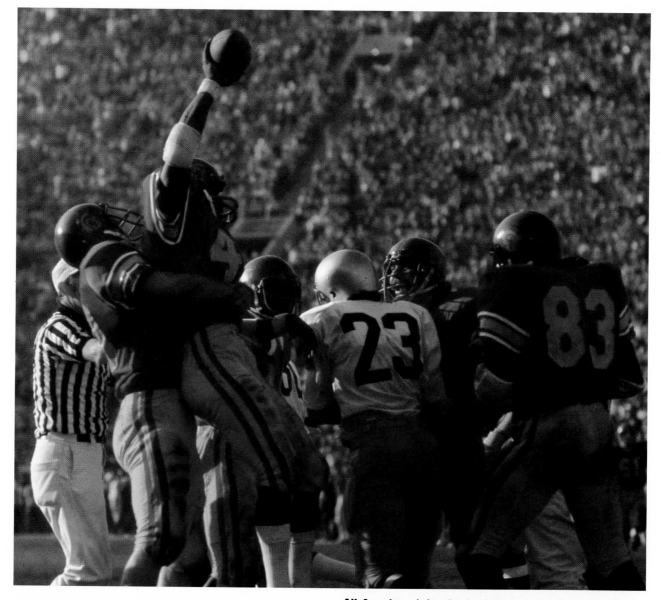

All-American defensive back Charles Phillips gets a lift from unidentified teammates after scoring on a 58-yard pass interception against Notre Dame in 1974.

A big reason for USC's improvement from 1975 to 1976 was the improvement of quarterback Vince Evans, shown in action against Notre Dame. Benefiting from John Robinson's emphasis on the quarterback position, Evans improved from 695 yards passing and a dismal 31.3 percent completion rate to a 53.7 percent rate for 1,440 yards and 10 TDs.

Paul McDonald had a great day against Notre Dame in 1978, throwing for two touchdowns as USC built a 24-6 lead. But perhaps his biggest pass came after the Irish had rallied to lead, 25-24, with 46 seconds remaining. USC's all-time leading passer hit Calvin Sweeney for 35 yards to move the Trojans into position for a game-winning field goal attempt.

school pal. The scoreboard went on the blink trying to keep up with the touchdown landslide.

There was more to come.

Before two minutes had elapsed in the fourth quarter, Haden had thrown a 16-yard scoring pass to Shelton Diggs and safety Charles Phillips had scored on a 58-yard pass interception.

The numbers and accomplishments were outstanding:

• USC scored 35 points on Notre Dame in the third quarter and 49 points, seven touchdowns, in less than 17 minutes of the second half.

• Davis set an NCAA career record for touchdown kickoff returns with six and, more significantly, he scored 11 touchdowns on Notre Dame in his USC career.

• The 55 points scored on Notre Dame were only four short of the record 59-0 blitz by the Blanchard-Davis Army team in 1944. McKay could have established a new opponent's record if he hadn't substituted liberally in the fourth quarter.

• Haden completed 11 of 17 passes for 225 yards and four touchdowns, equaling a school record for most scoring passes in a game.

McKay tried to sort things out after the game, saying, "I can't understand it. I'm gonna sit down tonight and have a beer and think about it. Against Notre Dame? Maybe against Kent State . . . but *Notre Dame?*"

Just a sampling of what the USC-Notre Dame series is all about.

There are other games and moments: Russ Saunders' 96-yard kickoff touchdown run in the 1929 game won by Notre Dame, 13-12 . . . unheralded Bucky O'Connor's amazing running show in Notre Dame's 27-0 shocker over USC in 1930 . . . Bud Langley's 96-yard touchdown on a pass interception with a referee inadvertently providing interference, in the 13-13 tie in 1936 . . . Ollie Day's late, first half touchdown pass to Al Krueger in USC's 13-0 upset win in 1938 . . . the performances by Jon Arnett and C.R. Roberts that offset Paul Hornung's brilliant game in USC's 42-20 win in 1955 . . . O.J. Simpson's big game in USC's 24-7 victory at South Bend in 1967 . . . the Trojan's shocking 38-28 win in 1970 even though Joe Theismann passed for 526 yards, a Notre Dame school record . . . Frank Jordan's winning field goal, 27-25, for USC with two seconds left in 1978 . . . and whatever the future might hold.

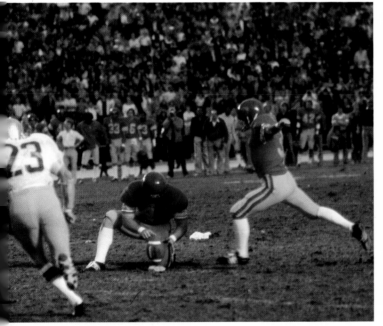

1978 USC vs. Notre Dame
Time Remaining, :02
Score: Notre Dame 25
**   USC   24**

1978 USC vs. Notre Dame
Time Remaining, :00
Score: USC   27
**   Notre Dame 25**

143

"The noblest Trojan of them all." There were other outstanding Trojan running backs in Morley Drury's era, but he was the true precursor of the now legendary USC tailback. His 223 carries for 1,163 yards was almost unheard of in his day. No Trojan would carry the ball so much or break 1000 yards until Mike Garrett in 1965, 38 years later. Drury was also a good passer, kicker and devastating defender. In an incredible two-way performance against Stanford in 1927, he paired 163 yards rushing with five interceptions. No wonder Drury's nickname is one that has never faded away.

Chapter Eight
NOBLE TROJANS, ALL

No one is sure at USC whether the man makes the position or the position makes the man. But one thing is certain. There is a mystique about the Trojan tailback that has endured for half a century.

A national magazine once described the USC tailback as a lineal figure, almost royalty.

Those who have held the scepter — the Garretts, the Simpsons, the Davises, the Bells and the Whites — became the most glamorous figures in college football.

Garrett, who was USC's first Heisman Trophy winner in 1965, recalled what it was like to be a Trojan tailback.

"I think it can be compared to other sports only in the most abstract ways. Perhaps becoming a USC running back is like playing for the New York Yankees in their great years with Babe Ruth, Lou Gehrig, Joe DiMaggio and Mickey Mantle. It's the only chance you get in your lifetime to put your act together, to feel like the chosen one.

"It's a psychological high like I've never known since."

There are two distinct eras in the Trojan tailback tradition and Garrett is the link between them. The active running backs in the 20s and 30s, the Thundering Herd days of Howard Jones, were designated as quarterbacks because they called the plays. But they were single-wing tailbacks in execution.

This was the era of Mort Kaer, Don Williams, Morley Drury, Russ Saunders, Marshall Duffield, Gus Shaver, Orv Mohler, Homer Griffith, Cotton Warburton, Amby Schindler and Grenny Lansdell.

In the 50s, two tailbacks emerged who, except for circumstances, might be as famous as their modern counterparts. Frank Gifford, who would later become an All-Pro with the New York Giants, wasn't a tailback until his senior season in 1951 after playing "T" quarterback and defensive back. Jon Arnett was an All-American tailback in 1955, but played only half a season as a senior in 1956 because of Pacific Coast Conference penalties imposed against USC.

It wasn't until McKay became USC's coach in 1960 and installed his Power "I" formation

that the Trojan tailback, benefiting from more media exposure than his predecessors, became the prominent figure that he remains today.

Garrett was McKay's first outstanding tailback, a runner who reinforced McKay's belief in his Power "I" system. He was also USC's first 1,000-yard rusher since Drury in 1927.

Then O.J. Simpson came along and broke Garrett's career rushing records while playing only two season, 1967 and 1968. Anthony Davis (1972-74) took Simpson's record away. Ricky Bell, a two-year tailback (1975-76), couldn't catch Anthony Davis but passed O.J. Finally Charles White, with four seasons, 1976-1979, as a tailback, moved ahead of them all.

Clarence Davis (1969-70) maintained the standards expected of a Trojan tailback. Because he followed Garrett and Simpson, he probably didn't get the recognition he deserved.

The modern USC tailbacks are so esteemed that three of them — Garrett, Simpson and White — won the Heisman Trophy. Two of them, Anthony Davis and Bell, were runners up for the award.

Not only were they renowned running backs, but some of the plays that were called for them — "23 blast" and "28 pitch" — still part of the USC offense, are also familiar to college football fans. McKay had an appropriately descriptive name for the Trojan sweep — Student Body Right.

In 1927 when the USC student body was considerably smaller than it is today, the Trojans even then had a powerful running game. The power runner of the time, the first of the great USC running backs, was a big man — 6 feet, 185 pounds — for that era. Morley Drury was called "The Noblest Trojan of Them All" by Mark Kelly, a sportswriter for the Los Angeles Examiner. Unlike many other nicknames, Drury's didn't fade with the passage of time. Drury, now 75 and living in Santa Monica, is still identified by that title when he is introduced at gatherings.

Drury played every position in the backfield and was a safety on defense. It wasn't uncommon for him to play the entire 60 minutes.

He was a triple threat tailback. He ran, he passed and he kicked, although he seldom threw more than six passes a game.

Long-time Trojan fans still recall the standing ovation he received when he walked across the Coliseum field and into the dressing room for the last time in 1927. He had concluded his college career by rushing for 180 yards and scoring three touchdowns in a 33-13 victory over Washington.

Drury had a remarkable senior season. He carried the ball 223 times for 1,163 yards, a 5.2 average. And, in one game, he had 45 rushing attempts. It was 41 years before another Trojan tailback worked as hard — Simpson's 47 attempts in 1968.

There were other accomplished tailbacks after Drury — "Racehorse" Russ Saunders who stunned Pittsburgh with his passing in the 1930 Rose Bowl game and who became a model for the landmark Tommy Trojan statue on campus, Gus Shaver who was effective at quarterback or fullback, Orv Mohler who was a smart runner and signal-caller and Cotton Warburton, an exciting break-away runner and tenacious defensive player, although he was only about 5-feet-7-inches and 145 pounds.

The Trojans had the one-two tailback punch of Lansdell and Schindler in the late 30s. Jones said that Lansdell was one of the best all-around backs he ever coached. Schindler was distinguished for his punishing, high knee action as he ran.

Gifford played two undistinguished seasons under Jeff Cravath in 1949 and 1950. He didn't blossom until he became a tailback in

Morley Drury scores one of his three touchdowns in his final game against Washington. Drury ended his career in noble style by rushing for 180 yards and receiving an ovation that stopped the game for some four minutes.

Jess Hill's multiple offense in 1951. He was USC's total offense leader that season with 1,144 yards.

There have been few dissenters to the statement that Simpson is the greatest running back in Trojan history. But Arnett, who played in 1954 and 1955 and part of 1956, might have been the most exciting.

Arnett had the agility of a gymnast, which he was, and he could take a full blow, manage to stumble away, hand scraping the turf while he regained his balance, and he would run some more. He was an escape artist, a Houdini on the field. Some of his runs seemed to last for several minutes.

Arnett was at his best in an open field and he was especially dangerous returning punts and kickoffs. There was a keen sense of anticipation whenever he touched the ball because fans might see a run that couldn't be recreated by a choreographer, whether it was a 105-yard kickoff return or a sideline-to-sideline excursion for minimum yardage and maximum thrills.

A 5-foot-11-inch, 195-pound running back, he later played with distinction for the Los Angeles Rams and Chicago Bears. Arnett's career rushing average of 5.66 yards tops all the great Trojan runners. But he had only 237 rushing attempts in two full seasons (1954, 1955). Bell, Simpson and White had more carries in *one* season — 385, 383 and 374.

Arnett made an immediate impact on USC fans as a sophomore in 1954 when he broke open a September night game against Pittsburgh with three touchdowns, gaining 118 yards on 15 carries.

From Braven Dyer's game story: "There are

One reason for the Trojan tailbacks' strong running is the bag drill. The back, in this case Bruce Dyer, runs between parallel lines of coaches and players who throw blocking bags at the runner's legs trying to knock him off balance.

two exceptional features to Arnett's running. One is his ability to turn it off and on, zipping at full speed when he sees a hole, or the opportunity to smash through a small opening. The other is his agility and balance.

"Time and again it looked as if he would hit the turf, but all he did was stick out one hand, regain his balance and leave bewildered tacklers strewn behind him."

There wasn't another USC runner of Arnett's class until Garrett became a tailback from 1963 through 1965.

McKay had been experimenting with the "I" formation as early as 1961. In 1962, Willie Brown became USC's first "I" back. But Brown was so versatile that he also lined up on occasion at flanker or split end. It was Garrett who dotted the "I", a tailback whose successes set the standard for the great runners who followed him.

"As far as I know, I was the first coach to stand a running back up in the "T" formation," McKay said. "We had the quarterback under center, the fullback down in

Howard Jones produced a number of outstanding tailbacks in addition to Morley Drury. His last great one, whom he felt was one of the best for his combination of power and finesse, was Grenville Lansdell, shown here in the 20-12 win over Notre Dame in 1939. Lansdell earned All-American honors as he helped the Trojans to an 8-0-2 season.

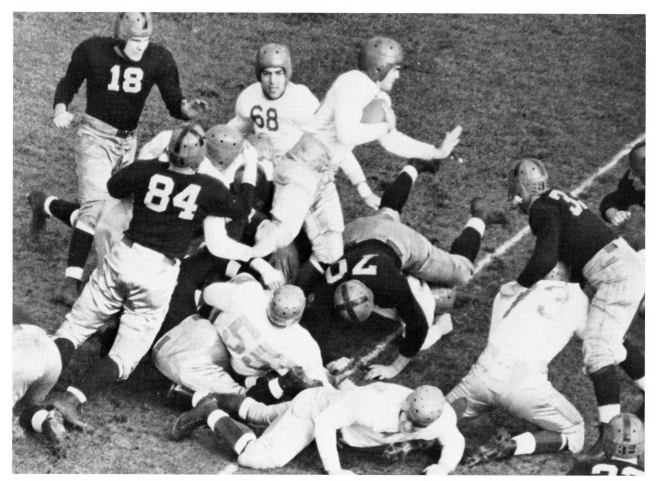

his stance several yards behind and the tailback, hands on knees, standing behind the fullback. We took the other halfback and made him a flanker or wingback.

"As he stands behind the fullback in the middle of the backfield, our tailback has a host of advantages, beginning with a tremendous number of angles to run from.

"He can run to either side of the center effectively, and the defense can't guess before the ball is snapped which direction he is going. He can get outside on a pitchout more quickly because he's already halfway across the backfield. In short-yardage situations we can crowd him behind the fullback, the leading blocker, and we can even swing him in motion more easily for passes.

"But, perhaps the most important advantage of all which we get by standing him up, is that he can see the defense before the play starts. We teach our tailbacks to study it every time they come out and line up. The phrase 'running to daylight' has become a cliche by now, and our backs do it, too. But they have a

The acrobatic Jon Arnett was perhaps the most exciting runner in USC history. Arnett amazed sportswriters, spectators, and opponents with his extraordinary balance and agility, skills nurtured through training in gymnastics.

head start against certain defenses because they know where the daylight is going to be."

Garrett was a stocky 5-feet-9-inches and 180 pounds and McKay said that he was the greatest college player he had ever seen at the time.

"Mike was a tremendously strong runner, so damn quick you couldn't believe it," McKay said. "He had much better speed than anyone ever thought he had. And when he was surrounded and going down, he could scramble along the ground for more yards faster than some people can run standing up. He was a good pass receiver, a very good blocker, a great faker and ran as well inside as he did outside."

In his three-year career, Garrett rushed for 3,221 yards, a new collegiate record; averaged 5.3 yards a carry; caught 36 passes for four more touchdowns and excelled as a punt and kickoff return specialist. He was the first Trojan tailback since Drury to become a workhorse, averaging 22 and 27 carries a game in 1964 and 1965 while gaining 948 and 1,440 yards. He was the nation's leading rusher in 1965, averaging 144 yards. That was also the year that he won the Heisman.

Garrett set the tone and practice style for USC tailbacks who followed him. In practice it was common for Trojan running backs to break through the line and then slow to a stop about 20 yards downfield. Not Garrett. Without being prodded, he ran out every play, 40 or more yards to the goal line.

"I felt that every time I ran the ball I was going to score," Garrett said. "So I would visualize it and practice like it was a break-away run. McKay said he liked what I was doing, but I didn't think anything more of it than it was helping me. After that, it became a tradition and, if you do it every day, it's not difficult at all. And you're so strong in the fourth quarter, it's unbelievable."

Dave Levy, a valued assistant coach under McKay for 16 years and a former USC assistant athletic director, recalled that when White was a freshman in 1976, he ran a play in practice and pulled up after six or eight yards.

"John Robinson called Charlie over and stood with him as Ricky Bell ran the next play," Levy said. "Bell ran 50 yards downfield. *That's* the way a USC tailback runs,' Robinson told White. Charlie never ran a short route again."

Garrett became a star running back with the

Mike Garrett, the first of the great modern tailbacks and USC's first Heisman Trophy winner (1965), breaks away as a UCLA defender gives futile chase.

A runner like Mike Garrett puts enough pressure on a defense without introducing the threat of a pass, but the tailback pass has been an effective, if sparingly used, weapon in USC's offensive arsenal.

"I think what impresses me the most about my playing years at USC is that it doesn't end once you stop playing. It's a life-long experience. It enhanced my understanding of myself as much as anything I can think of.

"An example of what I mean occurred after our 1965 loss to UCLA. We had UCLA really down in the third quarter and we were on our way to the Rose Bowl. But they came back and beat us, knocking us out of the Rose Bowl. You learn things at USC about winning and losing. I was really disappointed after the game. I'd lost my last chance to go to the Rose Bowl. I knew how happy the UCLA team and the fans were. I was heart-broken, but the worst thing I could have done, I felt, was detract from their win. That's one of the things Coach McKay believed in — win or lose, do it with dignity.

"I remember that I had tears in my eyes when I went over to the UCLA players. I told them, 'You guys played great and I know you'll do well in the Rose Bowl. Good luck to you.'

"The next week I was awarded the Heisman Trophy. I remember telling Coach McKay, 'I'd trade it all if our team could play in the Rose Bowl.' That's how much the game meant to me. But UCLA had beaten us. And they had come back to do it. They deserved the win and the Rose Bowl. That's part of what USC is all about: dignity, win or lose.

"The USC game that I remember most is one that no one else recalls. I was a sophomore and it was against Michigan State, the third game of the season, I think. It was the first time that I carried the ball a number of times. We had called a trap and when I got the ball, there was no hole. But I didn't panic, I slowed up to let the guard get there. He made his block and I broke through for yardage. I sort of orchestrated the play. I said to myself after the run, 'By golly, I can play with these guys.' In that game, which remains special to me, I gained a lot of confidence and I realized that I could play football in the major leagues."

Mike Garrett
Winner
1965 Heisman Trophy

Mike Garrett chews up a big chunk of his 3221 career yards against UCLA. At the time this was the NCAA career rushing record. For his day's work in his last UCLA game, Garrett netted 210 yards on 40 carries.

Kansas City Chiefs and San Diego Chargers. While he was making his mark in the NFL, a junior college transfer from San Francisco named Orenthal James Simpson enrolled at USC in 1967.

McKay had said that Garrett was the greatest college player he had ever seen. A few years later, without detracting from Garrett, McKay would be compelled to say that O.J. was the greatest.

"I never meant to imply anything derogative about Garrett, because he was a helluva football player," McKay said. "Simpson was just bigger (6-feet-2-inches, 207 pounds) and faster. O.J. accelerates like a jackrabbit, but his speed is deceptive, because he seems to glide. You don't think he's going fast until you try to tackle him. But how many big running backs have ever been on a world record relay team?"

Simpson, during his USC career, was on a 440-yard team that ran 38.6 seconds. And O.J., a legitimate 9.4 sprinter, just dabbled in track.

One of the more amazing aspects of Simpson's career is that he wasn't an experienced running back when he came to USC. He was a defensive back and then a flanker at City College of San Francisco, but he broke the national rushing and scoring records for junior colleges with 2,552 yards gained and 54 touchdowns in his two seasons.

Although Simpson was a raw talent, Dave Levy recalled O.J.'s first day in spring practice at USC.

"The first day we had him, I knew how good he would be. He looked like nothing I had ever seen before. We had him only nine days because he was told he could be on the track team. Well, in those nine days he made more long runs than all the tailbacks combined for the entire spring practice. But he fumbled a lot. However, when he came back in the fall, he didn't fumble. He just held the ball tighter."

Although USC lost only two games during the Simpson years, won the national

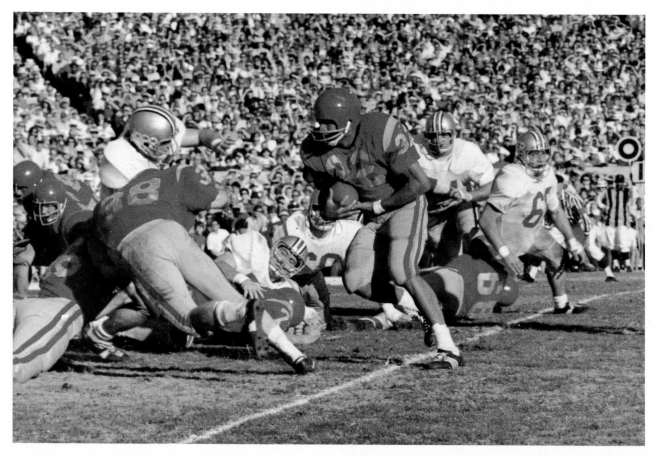

In the words of Northwestern coach Alex Agase, "He (O.J.) approaches the hole like a panther, . . .

championship in 1967 and played in two Rose Bowls, O.J. didn't have the supporting cast enjoyed by some other Trojan tailbacks.

There weren't any other menacing runners or a slick passing quarterback. So O.J. literally carried the load. He averaged 29 carries a game in 1967 and gained 1,543 yards. He stepped up his production in 1968 when he averaged 35 carries — twice peaking out at 47 — and accumulated 1,880 yards.

Simpson won the Heisman Trophy in 1968 by the most overwhelming margin in the history of the voting. That year he rushed for 1,709 yards during the regular season — an NCAA record. He also broke Garrett's career NCAA yardage record.

All this was accomplished in only two seasons and McKay was no longer criticized by writers and fans who thought that he was overworking Simpson.

To that line of questioning McKay once said, "We will continue to operate from only two plays which I'll signal to O.J. I'll nod 'run left,' or I'll nod 'run right.' And consider this: if you had Henry Aaron on your baseball team and the rules said he could take every turn at bat, wouldn't you let him?"

Simpson, like Garrett and later White, got stronger as the game progressed. Against Minnesota in 1968, USC trailed, 20-16, in the fourth quarter on a muddy field. O.J. carried on 11 of the last 12 plays, scored twice and the Trojans won, 29-20.

"Simpson," McKay said at the time, "gets faster in the fourth quarter and I get smarter."

People expected big games from O.J. and they were not disappointed. He scored three touchdowns against Notre Dame in 1967 as USC beat the Irish, 24-7, for its first victory at South Bend since 1939. His 40-yard touchdown run was the winning play against Oregon State, 17-13, in a 1968 game that was a virtual showdown for the Pacific 8 championship.

He is best remembered for his 64-yard

. . . and when he sees an opening, he springs at the daylight.''

ARNOLD FRANKEL

153

When I was looking at other schools and visiting other campuses, it was apparent to me that USC had a tradition of excellence. More than that, however, I sensed that the school cared about its past and its present. There was something special about the sports programs there, too. I got the feeling very quickly when I was there that I could become a part of something that would last.

The school has such a rich football history. When I was on the USC campus, the conversation might turn to Howard Jones. He'd coached over 25 years before I came. The students on campus were aware of who Morley Drury was and what he had done on the field. It was that kind of living tradition.

I think I very much needed to belong to something that had that kind of stability when I went to college. When you go to USC, you're a Trojan forever. It's something that lives. I played more than 10 years ago, but I'm still part of that tradition.

Running had been instinctive with me. Different players and different teams look at running, at attacking a defense intelligently, in different ways. McKay was able to cut through what a lot of others make complicated. With him, it came down to a few basics. So I was able to match my instinctive ability with the basics he taught. Then he gave me the opportunity to run.

Looking back over it all, my 64-yard touchdown run against UCLA in my junior year is still the highlight of my career. We beat them by one point, won a place in the Rose Bowl and won the national championship.

There was one other play that stands out more than others. We were playing Minnesota in 1968. We had been going with the same running play several times, and while I was gaining yardage, we were still behind. McKay called me over and told me, "Let's change it. Instead of hesitating at the hole for your blockers, from now on just flash by. Don't hesitate." The next time I got the ball, I didn't hesitate and I went 36 yards for a touchdown. We went on to win.

That's another part of what USC means. A lot of coaches at a lot of schools can prepare you before a game, but once on the field, there's little they can do. At USC, there's a constant improvement and work throughout the game. I think that's part of the USC tradition, too.

USC comes to camp with an edge. The players are better conditioned and better learned. They have the best coaching available. Their attitude toward football is so advanced. There's a real sense of being First Class.

All of that, I think, is part of what makes up the USC tradition.

O.J. Simpson
Winner
1968 Heisman Trophy

O.J. Simpson is in a class by himself, perhaps the greatest runner in college football history. He won the 1968 Heisman Trophy by the most overwhelming margin in the history of the voting. An unusual aspect of Simpson's style was his preference for wearing little or no hip pads, the better to feel a defender's hand and spin away before the tackler's grasp was secure.

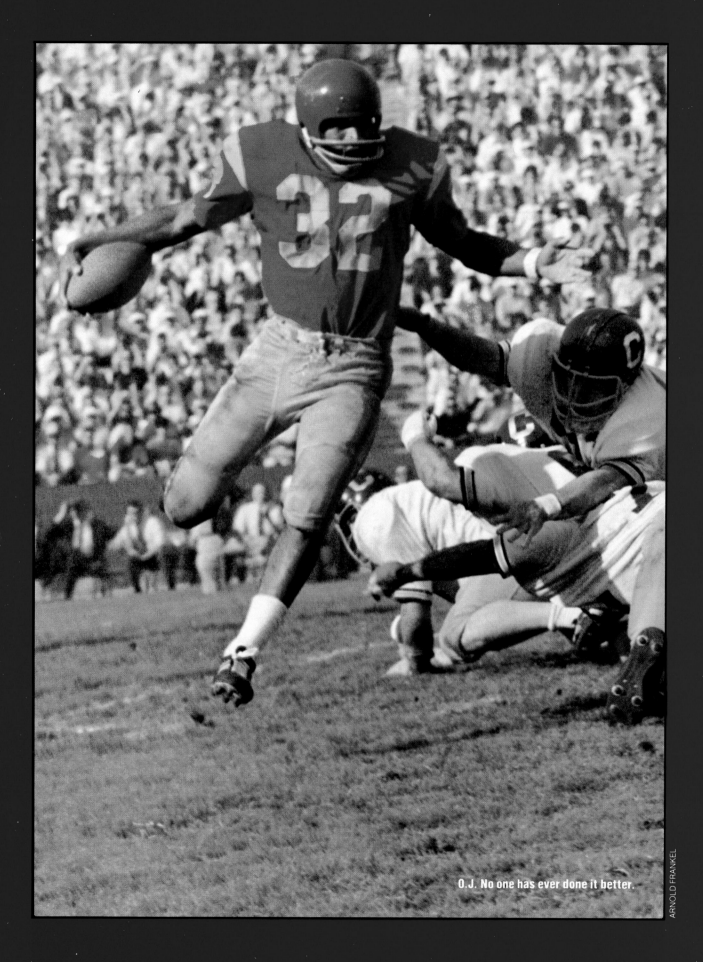

O.J. No one has ever done it better.

touchdown run in 1967 against UCLA in the fourth quarter on a "23 blast" when he faked right, cut left, eluded several Bruins and then broke free in the middle of the field. O.J.'s score and the subsequent conversion provided USC with a 21-20 win and the national championship.

Tommy Prothro, UCLA's coach at the time, said that an earlier run by O.J. in that game was the greatest he had ever seen. It was a modest 13-yard effort, but Simpson broke three or four tackles, kept surging and dragged Bruins across the goal line with him.

The affable and charismatic Simpson is one of football's all-time great runners. He became even more famous with the Buffalo Bills, setting an NFL single season rushing record of 2,003 yards in 1973. He concluded his 11-year pro career as the second leading NFL career rusher behind Jim Brown.

Of all the analogies about O.J., perhaps the one by Northwestern coach Alex Agase is

Clarence Davis (28) is sometimes called the forgotten tailback because he played right after Garrett and Simpson. Nevertheless he kept alive the tradition with an All-American performance. Leading the way is fullback Charlie Evans who kept alive another Trojan tradition that dates back to the days of Erny Pinckert — the great blocking back.

the most apt. "He approaches the hole like a panther," Agase said, "and when he sees an opening, he springs at the daylight."

Clarence Davis is sometimes called the forgotten USC tailback only because of timing. He was the tailback *after* Garrett and Simpson, both Heisman Trophy winners.

At 5-feet-11-inches and 195 pounds, he was bigger than Garrett and was a fast accelerating back who had all the necessary skills. Davis averaged 24 carries a game for his two seasons and gained 2,323 yards, but he didn't have the endurance of Garrett or Simpson.

USC was undefeated (10-0-1) in Davis' junior season and went to the Rose Bowl again, but slumped to a 6-4-1 record in 1970, which didn't help the tailback get media attention. He got more publicity later as a skilled runner with the Oakland Raiders.

The next Davis who played tailback at USC, Anthony, who was known as A.D., closely resembled Garrett in style and build. He stood

only 5-feet-nine-inches and weighed 190 pounds, but he had the stride of a taller man. McKay said A.D. had the ability to split himself like a Russian dancer and keep running. Some say his running form resembled a strutting drum major.

As a sophmore in 1972, Davis was a reserve tailback behind Rod McNeill at the outset of the season. But McNeill was struggling to come back from a hip injury. Davis kept improving.

A.D. became a late-season starter and gained 926 yards the last six games on his way to a 1,000-yard season. Included was his six-touchdown performance against Notre Dame.

Davis benefited from playing on a team that is considered the best in USC history and one of the great college teams of all time. The Trojans had a 12-0 record, won the national championship and concluded the season with an impressive 42-17 rout of Ohio State in the Rose Bowl.

Some people say that A.D. slipped a bit in 1973, when his rushing average was 4.0 compared to 5.8 in 1972. Still, he gained 1,112 yards and scored 15 touchdowns. He was more productive in 1974 with 1,421 yards for a career total of 3,724 yards, setting school and conference records.

Davis also excelled as a kickoff runner and has the second highest average, 35.1 yards, of all time. He also holds the NCAA record for most career touchdowns, six, on kickoff returns.

McKay has often said that A.D., who did knee dances in the end zone, was the brashest of his tailbacks. "He stopped me on campus one day and needled me about my weight," McKay says. "When most of my players saw me, they tried to avoid me."

Davis, unlike the other USC tailbacks of the modern era, didn't distinguish himself as a pro. He played for awhile in the Canadian Football League, was briefly with Tampa Bay, Houston and Los Angeles before he retired.

It would be misleading to say that whenever McKay needed a tailback, he simply searched

Anthony Davis' high stepping style made him USC's second leading career rusher. An All-American and Heisman runner-up, "AD" is the only one of USC's great tailbacks to play on two national championship teams, 1972 and 1974.

ARNOLD FRANKEL

157

With this carry against UCLA. Anthony Davis broke O. J. Simpson's career rushing record. A.D. still ranks second in career rushing and fifth in total offense. In addition he is USC's leader in most kickoff return categories and holds the NCAA record for kickoffs returned for touchdowns in a season (3) and in a career (6).

ARNOLD FRANKEL

high schools or junior colleges for the best running back and recruited him. Simpson was, at one time, a tackle in high school and later a flanker in junior college. Clarence Davis was a guard in high school. Anthony Davis was an All-City player at San Fernando High as a quarterback. Ricky Bell was a linebacker-fullback in high school, the positions he played at USC as a freshman and sophomore.

Levy, who has been associated with all the great USC tailbacks of the 60s and 70s, evaluated them:

"O.J. was in a class by himself. Garrett worked like a slave and was a combination of the Anthony Davis and Charlie White style in the way he attacked defenders. But White really attacks defenders. Garrett was probably faster than A.D. but not as fast as White. Bell didn't have their speed but he was a bull."

With A.D. gone, Bell was USC's tailback in 1975 and 1976. At 6-feet-2-inches and 218 pounds, he was bigger than his predecessors and ran over defenders as many times as he eluded them.

Bell recalls his first game as a starter, the 1975 opener against Duke. His stomach was a little queasy but he still ate a pregame steak. Then he joked with his teammates. Then he admitted that he was slightly nervous. Then he got sick.

"I was so nervous I couldn't think straight," Bell said. "I never felt like that before. All those great tailbacks that had gone before — Garrett, Simpson, Davis (C.D. or A.D.) — all that tradition I had to live up to."

Perhaps it is the mystique. Perhaps it is the belief that a man has to rise to the occasion because tradition demands it. In any case, Bell made a smashing debut, running for 256 yards — a single-game school record — and four touchdowns.

His teammates called him "Bulldog" because of a peculiar growling noise he made when he ran. The Bulldog chewed up everybody that season. He gained 1,875 yards for the regular season — the second highest total in NCAA history — and broke Simpson's all-time Pac-8 rushing record of 1,709 yards. And his 385 carries in 12 games were the most in USC history, edging Simpson's 383 for 11 games in 1968.

But it wasn't a satisfactory season for the Trojans. They had won their first seven games but then McKay made his announcement that he would be leaving USC for Tampa Bay the next year. USC lost four straight games and only partly salvaged the season by beating Texas A&M, 20-0, in the Liberty Bowl.

Robinson succeeded McKay in 1976 and Bell, an All-American in 1975, was now being touted as a Heisman Trophy candidate.

He seemed deserving of the award based on his play in a night game against Washington State at Seattle's Kingdome, where he rushed for 347 yards on 51 carries — the yardage only four short of the NCAA record and the attempts breaking Simpson's school record of 47 and the Pac-8 record of 50 held by Oregon State's Bill Enyeart.

Five games into the season Bell had accumulated 1,008 yards. But the sturdy tailback then had a series of injuries and he missed one game and parts of others.

When Bell was side-lined, a freshman from San Fernando High — Anthony Davis' old school — filled in commendably. Charles White, an All-City fullback as a prep player and a record-breaking hurdler in track, gained 858 yards in a backup role. He gained 114 of those yards in USC's 14-6 win over Michigan in the Rose Bowl.

The battered Bell settled for 1,433 yards. He was an All-American again, but Pittsburgh's Tony Dorsett won the Heisman.

Robinson has almost run out of adjectives in describing White who, in his four years at USC, surpassed all the rushing records of the other famous tailbacks.

He rushed for 1,478 yards as a sophomore, 1,859 as a junior and 2,050 as a senior. His career regular season total of 5,598 yards is the second highest in NCAA history.

He was an All-American and runner-up for the Heisman Trophy in 1978. He was the runaway winner in the Heisman balloting in 1979.

At 5-feet-11-inches and 185 pounds, he attacked defenders like a much bigger man. He was seldom injured, absolutely fearless and got stronger as games progressed.

"Charlie is the best football player in America," Robinson said at the outset of the 1979 season. "He's a fierce competitor who is both elusive and powerful as a runner, has great balance and vision, is an excellent receiver and is the most durable player I've ever coached.

"The other runners occasionally got tired. Charlie doesn't. I think he could play a doubleheader. He's the toughest player I've ever seen, too. If you're going to intimidate him, it might take you a month. You better bring your lunch with you . . . and your dinner.''

White was never better than in his final game for USC, the 1980 Rose Bowl against Ohio State. USC trailed, 16-10, with only a few minutes remaining. White became a wild man, gaining 71 yards on a 83-yard touchdown drive that he climaxed by jackknifing over the middle for a touchdown as the Trojans won, 17-16.

And there was the 1978 game against Alabama at Birmingham, where White gained 199 yards including a 40-yard touchdown run. After the game, which USC won, 24-14, in an upset, Barry Krauss, Alabama's All-America linebacker, lauded White.

''He is the best back I've ever played against. When we hit him, he still had momentum and, believe me, it was hard to get a good lick on him. He's quick, he's agile and he's powerful, and he explodes so fast it seems like he can break a long run any time.''

White is now exploding for the Cleveland Browns and Bell is playing for McKay at Tampa Bay.

Robinson said the USC tailback position is the single most identifiable position in college football. But skill alone cannot symbolize the Trojan tailback. He has been molded through long and arduous days of practice. He is a dedicated individual who is able to withstand pressure and performs at a high level of efficiency that the position demands of him.

''The person who plays tailback at USC has to be a strong person — like Charlie White — one who can accept responsibility,'' Robinson said. ''The tailback is kind of the heart of the team. He has to practice hard every day and be the kind of human being who can represent the school in a positive way.''

From Drury to White . . . from the 20s to the 80s . . . there is an unbroken line of USC tailbacks who are running through history. And making it, too.

Showing his awesome strength, Ricky Bell simply shrugs off a would-be tackler.

ARNOLD FRANKEL

While other USC tailbacks may have darted or flown, Ricky Bell rumbled. At 6-feet-2-inches and 218 pounds, he possessed the strength and endurance one would expect from a converted linebacker-fullback. Bell's 51 carries for 347 yards against Washington State in 1976, both school records, epitomized a career that twice brought All-American recognition as well as the runner-up slot in the 1976 Heisman Trophy race. A converted fullback, Bell began his career as a tailback by gaining 256 yards against Duke. He went on to break Simpson's single season record with 1,957 yards in his first year at the position.

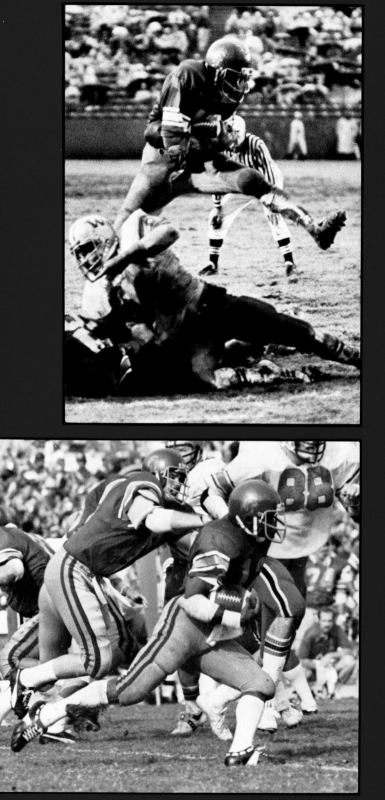

Going to USC and playing football there, with its tradition of great players in the past, was definitely the biggest stepping stone in my life from San Fernando High School.

It was a great challenge to me; not only in sports, but also in academics. I definitely sensed, very deeply, the feeling that I wanted to go to USC. When I was younger and then when I was playing at San Fernando, I heard about USC football and its winning tradition every Saturday when it played. It was nationally known for the kind of football teams and the kind of players that it developed.

I kept thinking to myself: if you call yourself the best, then you should go to the best.

There were a lot of thrills in playing for USC. But there are two that stand out for me as an individual. One was the opening game of the 1976 season against Missouri. I was a freshman and had replaced Bell. I made a 79-yard run for my first USC touchdown.

The bigger thrill for me, I think, was my last game in a USC uniform. That was in the 1980 Rose Bowl. We had about five minutes left to play in the game and we were losing, 16-10, to Ohio State. I was called on to do most of the running, I got some great blocks and I gained 71 of the 83 yards that we needed to score. Those runs were great thrills, but diving across the goal line for the final touchdown that enabled us to win was a tremendous way to end my USC career.

How did I feel about being named the Heisman Trophy winner? I sort of sensed that I had a good chance for it. I was playing that year behind a really superior USC line. But even though I had thought about the possibility of winning it, I wasn't ready when it was announced. It's hard to put into words what the Heisman means to me. Or what playing for USC has meant as a person and a football player.

Charles White
Winner
1979 Heisman Trophy

Charles White attacked defenses going over them or around them on the way to more than 6,000 career yards, (2,050 as a senior) and the Heisman Trophy. In his first game, he went 79 yards for a touchdown, launching a career that would make him the most prolific rusher in USC history (career and season).

Charles White put on perhaps the greatest one-man show in Rose Bowl history against Ohio State in 1980. He gained a record 247 yards including 71 and the TD on USC's late drive to victory.

Changing of the guard. On occasion in his senior year, Ricky Bell would move to fullback to block for a then-unknown freshman, Charles White.

The 1960s and 1970s were probably the most glorious of many glorious years for the USC tailback, the period being topped off by the all-time record setter, Charles White. The standard-bearer going into the 1980s is Marcus Allen. Like his predecessors, he will benefit from devastating blocking from his offensive linemen as demonstrated by Keith Van Horne.

ROBERT PARKER

Cinderella? He's not wearing glass slippers but Doyle Nave lived one of the all-time Cinderella stories. The fourth-string quarterback came off the bench to throw a touchdown pass in the closing moments to beat previously unbeaten, untied Duke in the 1939 Rose Bowl.

Chapter Nine
THE SHOWCASE GAMES

The Tournament of Roses, splashing the colorful pageantry of the parade into the excitement of the New Year's Day game, is regarded as one of America's most spectacular events.

Southern California is sometimes referred to as "Smogsville" by people in other parts of the country. But on January 1, that one special day of the year at least, the Pasadena air is clean and clear, the sun shines bright and the San Gabriel Mountains afford a magnificent backdrop for the countless millions watching the proceedings on television.

The Rose Bowl game is called the "Granddaddy" of all football bowl games. It is a very proper title. The first game was played in 1902 at Tournament Park and 65 other games have been played since.

USC, approximately 15 miles from Pasadena, regards the Rose Bowl as its second home. The Trojans have played in this prestigious game 23 times, accounting for almost one-third of the appearances by the Western representative.

USC usually wins on New Year's Day. The Trojans have a 17-6 record in the Rose Bowl and a 19-6 record for all bowl games — the most bowl wins and highest winning percentage (.760) of any team in history. To qualify for a ranking, a team must have played in at least 10 bowl games.

Exciting Rose Bowl games are commonplace and USC has contributed to this excitement from the 1923 team that beat Penn State, 14-3, to the 1980 team that rallied to defeat Ohio State, 17-16.

Leo Calland, Hobo Kincaid, Harold Galloway, Roy (Bullet) Baker, Russ Saunders, Erny Pinckert, Gus Shaver, Ernie Smith, Homer Griffith, Cotton Warburton, Doyle Nave, Al Krueger, Amby Schindler, Ray George, Norm Verry, Jim Hardy, Jim Callanan, Rudy Bukich, Al Carmichael, Des Koch, Aramis Dandoy, Pete Beathard, Hal Bedsole, O.J. Simpson, Bob Chandler, Sam Cunningham, Mike Rae, Anthony Davis, Pat Haden, Johnny McKay, Vince Evans and Charles White.

These names are just some of the Trojans who have enriched the historic Rose Bowl by their achievements.

Some of the games that stand out because of their significance or the unusual, thrilling

In the first Rose Bowl played in the present stadium, USC downed Penn State, 14-3. The fine running of Roy Baker and Gordon Campbell was the key to the Trojans' offense. Here Baker (33) follows Campbell (3) through the right side of the line.

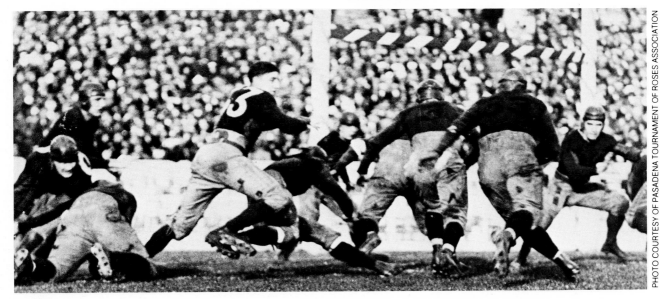

nature of the confrontation:

1923 — The Trojans had the distinction of playing in the Rose Bowl twice in the same season. The present Rose Bowl was built in 1922. USC and California inaugurated the new stadium with a regular season game. Cal won, 12-0, but declined an invitation to play in three straight Rose Bowl games.

So Gloomy Gus Henderson's team, which had won nine of its 10 games while scoring 222 points to the opposition's 28, was voted into the Rose Bowl by the Pacific Coast Conference.

Reversing tradition, Penn State had been invited long before the Trojans got their bid.

Penn State was coached by Hugo Bezdek, whose teams were undefeated in 1919, 1920 and 1921, but had lost three games in 1922. Bezdek had also coached an Oregon team that defeated Pennsylvania, 14-0, in the 1917 Tournament of Roses Game and the Mare Island Marines, who beat Camp Lewis, 19-7, the following year at Pasadena.

Henderson had an outstanding blocking combination in end Leo Calland and blocking back Hobo Kincaid; two effective quarterbacks, Chet Dolley and Harold Galloway, and a proven running back, Roy (Bullet) Baker.

But the story of the 1923 Rose Bowl is not so much what happened during the game but what happened *before* the game when the rival coaches, Henderson and Bezdek, almost got into a fight.

The game was to start at 2:30 p.m. The Trojans were on the field warming up when they learned that the Penn State team had been caught in a traffic jam and would be late.

At 3:15 Henderson was informed by the Penn State manager that the team had arrived. The USC coach went onto the field, where he found Bezdek standing alone.

"Is your first team here?" Henderson asked.

"No," Bezdek said.

"Your manager said the whole team had arrived," Henderson said.

"You can't call me a liar," Bezdek roared. "Take off your glasses and we'll settle the whole matter right here."

Henderson later said that he wasn't about to fight Bezdek, who had helped pay his way through the University of Chicago by fighting under an assumed name.

"I told him (Bezdek) that we would let our teams settle the issue," Henderson said. "I never saw Bezdek again to speak to in all my life, not even after the game."

The game began at 3:30 and the Nittany Lions took an early 3-0 lead. Then Galloway, the small USC quarterback, made what writers at the time said was "one of the greatest plays ever seen on a gridiron."

Baker threw a flat pass on fourth down at the

If Doyle Nave was Cinderella in the 1939 Rose Bowl, then Al Krueger was the prince. He caught four passes in a row from Nave, including the winning touchdown.

Penn State 10-yard line. The ball wasn't anywhere near the intended receiver but Galloway made a stretching leap for the ball, held onto it as he skidded on the turf and was knocked out as he was hit on the two-yard line.

Gordon Campbell scored on a delayed buck. In the second half, long runs by Baker and shorter thrusts by Campbell produced another USC touchdown.

The 14-3 victory was USC's first in the Rose Bowl and set the standard for future Trojan teams. The win also brought national recognition to the relatively small Methodist school in Los Angeles — and respect from the Eastern football establishment.

1930 — This was the first Thundering Herd team to play in the Rose Bowl and some historians say it was one of Howard Jones' best teams, even though the Trojans lost two games in the 1929 season, 13-12 to Notre Dame and 15-7 to California.

USC compiled 492 points in 1929 — still a school record — including one-sided victories over UCLA (76-0) in the first meeting between the crosstown rivals, Washington (48-0) and Carnegie Tech (45-13), an established Eastern power.

In "Racehorse" Russ Saunders, Jones had one of the most underrated running backs in the country, an athlete who was annoyed that he didn't make the All-American team. USC did have an All-American, end Francis Tappaan, and such outstanding players as blocking back Erny Pinckert, lineman Nate Barragar, the team's captain, end Garrett Arbelbide and fullback Gus Shaver.

USC's opponent was undefeated Pittsburgh, coached by the famous Jock Sutherland. They

Duke's defense proves why it was unscored on in 1938 with this crushing stop of USC's Mickey Anderson.

had imposing credentials. The Panthers had four All-Americans: end Joe Donchess, guard Bob Montgomery, halfback Toby Uansa and fullback John Parkinson.

Sutherland's pregame plan was to shut down Saunders, who had gained 124 yards against Carnegie Tech and had scored on a 96-yard kickoff return against Notre Dame. But Jones was now using the forward pass more frequently. He had beaten Stanford by passing in 1928 and repeated in 1929.

The Trojans, known for their vaunted running game, surprised Pitt by passing. Saunders threw two passes in the first 10 minutes of the Rose Bowl game. Both went for touchdowns — 55 yards to Harry Edelson and 25 yards to Erny Pinckert. Saunders threw another touchdown pass before the game ended. His record of three scoring passes in the Rose Bowl wasn't equaled until Jim Hardy, another USC quarterback, repeated the feat in the 1944 game against Washington.

The Trojans so dominated the Panthers that they led, 26-0, at halftime and 33-0 in the second half on the way to a 47-14 rout — the most one-sided win in Rose Bowl history to that time.

Saunders wasn't the only Trojan back who took to air. Marshall Duffield passed effectively and, when the game ended, USC had gained 297 yards by passing — an astounding total for that era.

Saunders' passing was decisive but he also made another play that took the heart out of Pittsburgh. Uansa swept end on the first play of the game and appeared headed for a touchdown. Saunders, initially knocked down on the play, regained his feet, chased Uansa and brought him down at the USC 14-yard line, ending a 68-yard run. But Pitt didn't score and USC took charge of the game.

Walter Eckersall, a former All-America quarterback and a noted football authority, wrote after the game: "Better football is played on the Pacific Coast than in any other section of the country."

Pop Warner, Stanford's coach, commented: "Never have I seen a game so dominated by the forward pass."

It was the first of Jones' five winning appearances in the Rose Bowl and, perhaps, the most impressive.

1939 — USC followed its 47-14 win over Pittsburgh with a 21-12 victory over Tulane and 35-0 thrashing of Pitt in the 1932 and 1933 Rose Bowl games.

But USC slumped from 1934 through 1937, winning only 17 of 42 games with six ties.

By 1938, Jones had apparently assembled another strong team, although it wasn't apparent in the season opener when USC was shocked by Alabama, 19-7, at the Coliseum.

The Trojans were upset by Washington, 7-6, later in the season but they earned the Rose Bowl bid by defeating strong California, 13-7, and enhanced their prestige by upsetting Notre Dame, 13-0, and knocking the Irish out of the national championship.

Grenny Lansdell, Jack Banta, Ray George, Bill Fisk, Phil Gaspar, Bob Hoffman, Jimmy Jones, Bob Peoples, Harry (Blackjack) Smith, Ben Sohn, Bob Winslow, Joe Shell, Howard Stoecker, John Stonebraker, Ray Wehba, Don McNeil, Mickey Anderson and Ollie Day were some of the prominent members of that team. There were also a fourth-string quarterback, Doyle Nave, and a sophomore end, "Antelope" Al Krueger, who would become memorable whenever fans talked about Rose Bowl games.

There was considerable pressure upon USC

The expression on the face of Duke's Eric Tipton (20) says it all as Al Krueger hauls in Doyle Nave's pass for a 7-3 USC win in the 1939 Rose Bowl. Incredibly, Duke had played ten games and 59 minutes without giving up a point until Nave and Krueger's miracle finish.

to invite undefeated Texas Christian to the Rose Bowl. The school, at that time, made the selection of the Eastern representative. The Horned Frogs and their boosters campaigned blatantly for the bid, and one prominent Texan even sent turkeys as Thanksgiving Day presents to Los Angeles sportswriters.

TCU, led by Heisman Trophy-winning quarterback Davey O'Brien and center Ki Aldrich, was indeed a logical choice. But USC officials were indignant that TCU had so brazenly sought the bid.

So USC, resisting the Texas pressure, invited Duke. The Blue Devils had beaten Pittsburgh and were undefeated, untied and unscored upon.

Wallace Wade, who had coached Alabama to two previous victories in the Rose Bowl and a tie with Stanford, had more than a representative team. Eric Tipton was a great

punter who would conservatively kick on first down in his own territory; Dan Hill was an outstanding center and Duke had an impregnable defense.

The Duke defense lived up to its billing in the Rose Bowl game as it thwarted every USC scoring threat. The Blue Devils led, 3-0, on Tony Ruffa's field goal early in the fourth quarter.

With Lansdell at tailback, USC began to drive late in the game, reaching the Duke 34 with two minutes remaining. It was at this juncture that Nave, a fourth-string quarterback behind Lansdell, Anderson and Day, came into the game.

There are conflicting reports on how Nave, who had played a total of only 35 minutes and 22 seconds during the regular season, got to play.

The popular story as detailed in Joe

Jim Hardy hands off to John Evans in USC's 29-0 thumping of Washington in 1944. Hardy was a thorn in the Huskies side all day throwing three touchdown passes to tie Russ Saunders' record. This game was an unusual match up of two west coast teams due to the travel restrictions imposed by the war. It was also the first of four Rose Bowl appearances in five years for Jeff Cravath's Trojans of the 1940's.

PHOTO COURTESY OF PASADENA TOURNAMENT OF ROSES ASSOCIATION

171

Hendrickson's book, *The Tournament of Roses, a Pictorial History of the Rose Bowl,* is that Joe Wilensky, an assistant coach operating a phone from the bench and relaying messages from assistants in the press box, faked a phone call.

The coaches upstairs had reportedly left to join the team on the field but Wilensky grabbed the phone and said, "Yes, yes — I get it. I'll tell him right away." His voice was loud enough for everyone on the bench to hear. Then Wilensky told athletic director Bill Hunter that the word was to send in Nave and have him pass to Krueger and to relay the message to Jones.

Nave overheard the information and rushed into the game without waiting for Jones to send him in. Al Wesson, USC's publicity director at the time, discounts this story and says that Jones had planned to put Nave into the game if USC was in scoring position because he was the team's best passer.

When Nave went in, the ball was on the 39, not the 34, as USC had incurred a five-yard penalty for too many time-outs. Nave's first pass went to Krueger for a 13-yard gain to the Duke 26. His second pass to Krueger was a strike to the Blue Devil 17. The next pass to Krueger lost two yards.

Then, Nave faded to his 31-yard line, waited for Krueger to outmaneuver Tipton and threw a perfect pass to his favorite receiver in the corner of the end zone on a pattern called "27 down and out."

Four straight passes and Duke's goal line had been crossed for the first time that season. Gaspar added the anticlimactic extra point and USC had remarkably won, 7-3.

One of the ironical twists to the game is that

PHOTO COURTESY OF THE PASADENA TOURNAMENT OF ROSES ASSOCIATION

Hal Bedsole, a 6-foot-5-inch wide receiver, goes high to grab one of his two touchdown receptions behind two Wisconsin defenders in the 1963 classic.

Pete Beathard lowers his head, powering into a Wisconsin defender. Ben Wilson (49) provides blocking support on Beathard's flank.

Like a couple of hornets, Pete Beathard (12) and Willie Brown (26) attack Wisconsin's All-American end, Pat Richter, bring him down, and strip him of the ball.

Dyer had editorially urged Jones to "give my boy Doyle Nave a chance" all season. But Dyer, Nave's No. 1 supporter, left the game *before* the fourth-stringer threw his four historic passes.

A few years later, when Nave was in the Navy serving in the South Pacific, he met Dan Hill, who captained the Duke team and they rehashed the game.

"When I came into the game did you have an idea that I was going to pass?" Nave asked Hill.

"Hell, no, we didn't even know who you were," Hill replied.

Nave didn't have enough playing time to earn a letter during the 1938 season. But the USC athletic board made an exception and voted Nave his letter — without prompting.

1963 — As USC's coach, John McKay made eight visits to the Rose Bowl and could be excused if he didn't remember the details of every game. But he has total recall of his first appearance there.

The 1963 game is still called one of the most dramatic and one of the most bizarre in Rose Bowl history. USC, undefeated national champion, was matched against Wisconsin, the Big 10 champion who had lost one game and was ranked No. 2 in the country.

The ideal pairing.

Despite the Trojans' ranking and record, Milt Bruhn's Badgers were a two-point favorite. The odds seemed out of line for more than three quarters as USC, behind the passing combination of quarterback Pete Beathard and Hal Bedsole, opened up a 42-14 lead. Beathard had thrown a record four touchdown passes, two being caught by Bedsole, the 6-foot-5-inch receiver.

No one to this day is quite sure how the

This is what the Rose Bowl is all about: the best against the best. USC All-American Gary Jeter battles Ohio State All-American John Hicks.

momentum switched. Some say that Wisconsin quarterback Ron VanderKelen simply got hot. Others say that USC let down. McKay contends that injuries to some of his key linemen finally took their toll and prevented USC from pressuring VanderKelen.

There was an added twist to the game. The officials were accused of over-officiating.

The game lasted a record three hours and five minutes, prompting Los Angeles Times columnist Jim Murray to write: "The game lasted only slightly longer than the War of 1812. If the game had lasted one more quarter, they would have run into next year's Rose Bowl traffic."

The length of the game presented an additional problem. Rose Bowl lights were not adequate and the teams played part of the fourth quarter in semidarkness.

VanderKelen, however, lit up the scoreboard. He completed 18 of 22 passes in the fourth quarter and 33 of 48 for the game for 401 yards. When he threw a 19-yard scoring pass to end Pat Richter with 1:19 remaining, Wisconsin had narrowed USC's lead to five points, 42-37. The Badgers had scored 23 points in 12 minutes. The Trojans were barely hanging on.

Ohio State's two-time Heisman winner Archie Griffin finds the going rough against USC's swarming defense in the 1975 Rose Bowl.

If Wisconsin had won, considering the deficit the team had to overcome, it would have been a near-miracle. As it turned out, USC recovered a Wisconsin on-side kick and ran out the clock for a 42-37 victory.

The offensive portion of the Rose Bowl record book was almost rewritten after this game. VanderKelen set passing records for most attempts, completions and yardage; Beathard for touchdown throws; Richter for receptions (11); Wisconsin for first downs (32); and both teams for combined most points (79).

Some of McKay's players were dejected after the game, stunned by the Wisconsin comeback. McKay tried to revive his team's spirits in the dressing room.

"Wisconsin," he spat it out like a swear word. "That's all they're talking about. In a few minutes the writers will be in here telling you men how lucky you were to pull this one out. Don't you believe it. You're the best damn team I ever saw. Our intention was to win today — and what does the scoreboard say?

"Who was picked to lose to the Big 10 powerhouse? We were. Ask the experts which team scored 42 points. You did, and you earned every one of them. We came in No. 1. They came in No. 2 and lost. That makes us still No. 1."

Some USC players were still depressed. In Ken Rappoport's book, *The Trojans, a Story of Southern California Football,* Bedsole was quoted as saying:

"There was no feeling of elation for winning the national championship. It was really unfortunate. It was discouraging after they came back like that. All the stories in the papers were about the great Wisconsin comeback. We felt we were national champions before the Wisconsin game and we knew we were far superior than the Badgers. And we should have won by more. But that comeback took a lot out of us."

1975 — McKay had been called a riverboat gambler because he seldom played conservatively when a game was on the line. But his luck had been bad in two-point conversion attempts.

Three previous times in his coaching career he had gone for two-point conversions, instead of going for a tie and he had lost — including a 14-13 setback to Purdue in the 1967 Rose Bowl.

But he made a two-point roll one more

time . . .

By the mid-70s Ohio State and coach Woody Hayes had become accustomed to Rose Bowl invitations. Hayes' 1955 team had beaten USC, 20-7; Ohio State edged Oregon, 10-7, in 1958, and beat USC again, 27-16, in 1969.

But Woody lost his touch against the Pacific 8 schools. His Buckeyes were upset by Stanford, 27-17, in 1971. They were routed by USC, 42-17, in 1973. He rebounded with a 42-21 win over the Trojans in 1974.

Another USC-Ohio State matchup, the rubber game in the series of the 70s, awaited in 1975. The teams had similar records. USC was 9-1-1, Ohio State 10-1. The Buckeyes were ranked No. 2 in the UPI coaches' poll, the Trojans fourth.

The game figured to be close. It was close, but it wasn't a classic encounter. Both teams squandered scoring opportunities with untimely turnovers — four for USC, three for OSU.

USC led twice at 3-0 and 10-7 before Ohio State, guided by clever running quarterback Cornelius Greene, took the lead at 17-10 midway through the fourth quarter.

With time running out, USC had the ball on its own 17-yard line. It was catch-up time. Usually accomplished by passing.

McKay, who called the plays, displayed a cool hand. He had quarterback Pat Haden hand off to substitute tailback Allen Carter, then fullback Dave Farmer for substantial gains. Carter had replaced All-American tailback Anthony Davis, who was forced to leave the game in the first half with a chest injury.

The Trojans stayed on the ground to Ohio State's surprise. They worked the ball to the Buckeye 38 before McKay changed his strategy. Haden threw his first pass of the drive, a 38-yard scoring throw to Johnny McKay, the coach's son, who beat an Ohio State defender on a corner pattern.

The Trojans now trailed, 17-16. Fans wondered whether McKay would finally quit bucking the odds and go for a tie with a one-point conversion. They should have known better.

Haden rolled out, planning to run. He was shut off on the outside. So he improvised. He threw a low pass to flanker Shelton Diggs in the end zone. Diggs went to the ground to make the catch with 2:03 remaining. McKay had drawn to an inside straight.

USC held off Ohio State in the waning

This sequence shows one of the biggest plays in Rose Bowl history, this time in the 1975 game against Ohio State. With 2:03 remaining, Pat Haden ended an 83-yard desperation drive with this 38-yard touchdown pass to Johnny McKay to pull USC within one point of the Buckeyes at 16-17.

Following the big TD pass, Shelton Diggs makes a diving catch of Haden's pass for the two-point conversion as McKay (25) and the crowd exult in the 18-17 win. The victory wrapped up the fourth national title for young McKay's father.

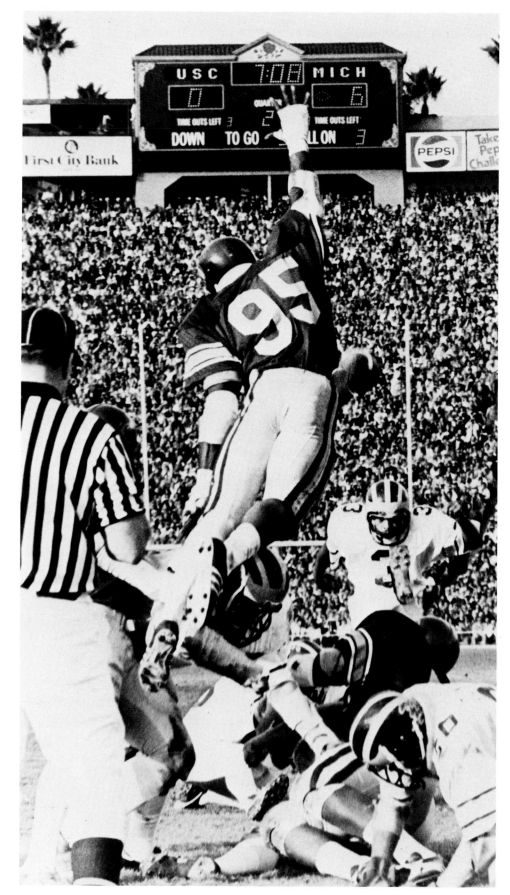

Michigan scored first in the 1977 classic, but Walt Underwood grabbed the momentum back for USC with this soaring block of the extra point attempt. The Trojan defense shut off the Wolverines the rest of the way in a 14-6 win.

minutes to win, 18-17.

McKay's gamble had earned more than just a Rose Bowl victory. Notre Dame beat No.1 ranked Alabama that night in the Orange Bowl and USC moved from fourth to first in the UPI poll to get a share of the national championship.

"No, I never even thought about not going for two points," said McKay later in the dressing room. "We *always* play it that way. Always have, always will."

There have been memorable moments for USC in the Rose Bowl and some heartbreaks too:

Best one-man show: Tailback Charles White, who beat Ohio State (17-16) in the closing minutes of the 1980 game. He gained 71 yards on an 83-yard ground assault. He charged through a huge hole at right guard for 32 yards, then swept end for 28 yards. He took a breather and then returned to the game to slam for three, five and two yards and a first down just short of the goal line. From there he soared over the middle for a touchdown.

For the game, he gained 247 yards on 39 carries to break Rose Bowl records for rushing yardage and attempts.

Most humiliating defeats: 34-14 to Alabama in 1946 for USC's first Rose Bowl loss after eight straight victories and 49-0 to Michigan in 1948.

Most satisfying win: Several games fall in this category, including USC's 7-0 victory over Wisconsin in 1953. Reserve quarterback Rudy Bukich threw a 22-yard scoring pass to halfback Al Carmichael in the third quarter.

It held up, providing the Pacific Coast with its first victory over a Big 10 team since the Rose Bowl pact between the conferences had been originated in 1947.

Craziest run: USC's Aramis Dandoy crisscrossed the field several times on an 88-yard punt return for a touchdown in 1955 as Ohio State beat USC in the mud and rain.

Quickest touchdown: USC end Jim Callanan blocked a punt and scored in the opening 90 seconds of the game against Tennessee in 1945 — a Rose Bowl record.

Jones' last hurrah — Tennessee came into the 1940 Rose Bowl on the crest of a 23-game win streak. But the Vols were no match for Howard Jones' last great team. The Trojans, led by hard-running Amby Schindler, won easily, 14-0.

After the game, Henry McLemore of the United Press, wrote: " . . . There is a lesson to be learned from this Rose Bowl game. There is no sense in betting on a team that buys its clothes in the boys' department to beat a team (USC) that has to shave twice a day and is fitted for suits in the adult or grown up section."

Biggest surprise: Saunders' passing against Pittsburgh in the 1930 game and Pinckert's running against Tulane in the 1932 game. Pinckert, who made All-American as a blocking back, scored twice on end runs of 30 and 23 yards.

The Rose Bowl. It has been USC's showcase game since the early 20s.

A most valuable smile. With Ricky Bell knocked unconscious on USC's first possession, much of the offensive burden in the 1977 Rose Bowl fell to quarterback Vince Evans. He responded brilliantly and took home the MVP trophy.

With the score USC 7, Michigan 3 in 1979, Charles White soars toward the goal line. The play is one of the most controversial in Rose Bowl history. The officials signaled touchdown; the Wolverines howled fumble. Thanks to this photograph, the reader can judge for himself.

This time there is no doubt as Charles White culminates
the greatest one-man show in Rose Bowl history by
jack-knifing over the Ohio State goal line to tie the score at
16 with 1:39 remaining. The extra point capped a great
comeback and an undefeated season in 1979. And White's
performance added another legend to The Trojan Heritage.

SPIRIT
OF TROY

PUBLISHER'S NOTE

First, we express our appreciation and thanks to Dr. Richard H. Perry, USC's director of intercollegiate athletics. Without his initial interest in this project and his continued enthusiastic support, this volume would not have been possible.

To Bob Boyd, USC's associate athletic director, and Ted Tompkins, assistant to the athletic director, we are indebted for their assistance in the overall coordination of the entire project.

Our thanks go, too, to USC's sports information director Jim Perry and his staff — Dennis Kirkpatrick, Tim Tessalone and Nancy Mazmanian — for allowing us access to their files, for assisting us in gathering most of the photographs in this book and for providing information on many of the players and the games.

Buddy Dyer and the Citizens Savings Athletic Foundation in Los Angeles provided help in gathering some of the photographs, particularly those of the early eras. Their cooperation has helped to make this book a complete pictorial record of USC football.

Thanks to photographers Robert Parker and Arnold Frankel who provided color pictures from their private collections for inclusion in this book.

Thanks also go to Ed Pierce, public relations director of the Pasadena Tournament of Roses Association, for allowing us access to his photographic files.

We are indebted to Frank Bradley of Virginia Beach for his assistance in writing many of the captions.

JCP Corp. of Virginia
Virginia Beach, Virginia
October 1980

All photographs in this edition are courtesy of USC Sports Information except as noted.